A PEOPLE'S HISTORY
OF
COFFEE AND CAFÉS

OTHER BOOKS BY BOB BIDERMAN

Coffee! Stories of Extreme Caffeination
Eight Weeks in the Summer of Victoria's Jubilee
A Knight at Sea
Sacha Dumont's Amsterdam
Strange Inheritance
Genesis Files
Judgement of Death
Paper Cuts
Mayan Strawberries
Letters to Nanette
Red Dreams
Koba
TechnoFarm
Anna and the Jewel Thieves (with David Kelley)
The Polka-Dotted Postman (with Cat Webb)
Further Education
Romancing Paris. Again.
Left-Handed Portuguese Zen

A PEOPLE'S HISTORY
OF
COFFEE AND CAFÉS

BOB BIDERMAN

BLACK
APOLLO
PRESS

First published in Great Britain by
Black Apollo Press, 2013

Paperback ISBN: 9781900355780
Hardback ISBN: 9781900355773

A CIP catalogue record of this book is available at the British Library.

A website has been set up as a companion to this book containing an extensive coffee bibliography along with images, charts, maps, statistics and discussions. It can be accessed at: www.blackapollopress.com/coffee.html.

Cover Design: Kevin Biderman
Cover Image: Le Café du Bel Air, Koloriete Radierungen

The author wishes to express his thanks to Cat Webb for the research she did on this project some twenty years ago; to Kevin Biderman who helped develop Café Magazine, without which this book could never have come to fruition; to David Cutting, who read, advised and corrected; and to Joy Magezis, who was there from the very beginning and kept the fires burning till the very end. It couldn't have been done without you.

CONTENTS

The Coffee Bearer, John Frederick Lewis, 1857.
City of Manchester Art Galleries

PREFACE

IT WAS AS a student at the University of California in Berkeley during the early 1960s that I first succumbed to coffee's special allure and its portal into a more adult world of exotic pleasures. Up till then coffee had simply been a drink that one bolted down in the morning in order to wake up. Taken from a vacuum-sealed can, boiled in a percolator pot, consumed with lots of milk and sugar to moderate the bitterness, it tasted awful but its effect was necessary in order to approach lucidity after a series of endless nights and groggy dawns. Back then, coffee was java. The image was of a Hollywood Western where a lonesome cowboy stirred a spoonful of grounds into a dented pan of water boiling over a smoky campfire, then pouring the steaming brew into a tin cup and drinking it in the chilly mist under the rising sun. It wasn't supposed to taste good; it did its job and that was enough. But now, in this brand new decade when I had finally reached the age of maturity, coffee had become something else altogether. It wasn't only the drink – which suddenly did taste good – it was also the place where I drank it.

In the late 1950s and early 60s the San Francisco Bay Area was bubbling up espresso, even though 99.9% of Americans didn't yet know how to spell it. First and foremost in spreading this new café culture (to me, anyway) was the Café Trieste in North

Beach. There the ex-pat Italian community, nurtured on coffee and Puccini, met the new bohemia that coupled the re-discovery of this formerly prosaic drink with an angst-driven homage. Walking down Columbus Avenue in those days you couldn't help but be immersed in and consumed by the deeply rich and caramelized fragrance that came belching forth from the North Beach coffee roaster, Graffeo's. It all mixed so well with the chilly turquoise waters blending into the cadmium skies – viewed from the heights of the city's bohemian village and mirrored in a pastel mural painted lovingly on the inside wall at the Trieste by a beat artist trying to merge his fantasy of an Italian fishing village with an even more fantastic notion of a primordial San Francisco.

The two cafés I was most familiar with back then were the Café Med in Berkeley and the Café Trieste. Even though they both were run by people who came from the Italian café tradition, they had a very different clientele and ambience. Whereas the Café Trieste was based in the Italian community of North Beach (the 'Little City'), the Med was of and for the independent students and resident bohemia who made Berkeley's Telegraph Avenue their universal font providing everything from books to bagels. The Med was their home from home either in the morning, afternoon or evening (often merging into one) and within its walls, competing with the constant hiss and steam of the two magnificently polished espresso machines that sat like triumphant sculptures before some Delphic temple, infinite discussions, debates, discourses, rants, confessions and manifestoes which would (perhaps) change the world for all time to come, took place amongst the innumerable sips, gurgles, and gulps of rich black espresso alone in a small porcelain cup or in a fluted glass mixed with a frothy white substance.

At the Trieste the drink was the same but the ambiance different. Here the immigrant Italians shared their space with the new wave of beatniks who ventured forth from places like City Lights Books, attracted by the ambrosia that somehow was made from the same plant that provided the beans for the grotty stuff that came from their percolator pots and allowed them to write another hour's worth of verbiage before either finding the Muse or drifting off into their own special Neverland. Unlike the Med, the Trieste of the early 60s was very much of and for the Italian community that had settled in North Beach some years before, but it was also a place that respected other people's art and culture (even if it came with long hair and a certain amount of grunge) as long as those who shared their space had a mutual respect and realised that the Trieste was primarily for the village residents.

The movement of the espresso culture outside the purview of the Italian community was slow in coming but followed the seismic cultural shift taking place in America and the consequent movement of bohemia to peripheral neighbourhoods. Based on models like the Trieste and the Café Med, these new cafés emphasised frothy drinks for those young Americans who found pure espresso too hard to handle.

It wasn't until later that I realised how much these two cafés – the Trieste and the Med – fit into the historical pattern of the coffeehouse that separated them from the bars, pubs and bistros immersed in the culture of alcohol. By then I had already been living in Europe for over a decade and had become interested in following the trail of this curious plant that provided the mental fuel for a new generation of google-eyed explorers now using it to brew up fantastic dreams inside magic boxes.

In 1983, I left San Francisco for England. At the time, getting a good cup of coffee in London meant either paying a fortune at a classy West End restaurant or hanging out with the continental Europeans in Soho. And yet if one went back only a few hundred years, the situation would have been quite different. London, in the 18th century, was probably the coffeehouse capital of the world with over 2,000 throughout the city. They flourished during a time of rapid economic transformation, becoming the focal point for new ideas that were sparking London's emergence as one of the most exciting places to be in the Western world. These coffeehouses were well stocked with books, newspapers and magazines, were buzzing with energy from morning till night and were open to all upon payment of a penny – and so they became known as 'Penny Universities'.

I began *Café Magazine* in the early 90s as a homage to a culture I found missing in contemporary Britain – out of a sense of nostalgia for things past but also as an attempt to recreate the idea of the café community and show how important it had been to the development of a vital, cutting-edge culture and politic; how the coffeehouse served as a cauldron in the synthesis of ideas that drew from many sources outside the mainstream institutions and how it served as a refuge for those artists, writers, musicians, philosophers and dreamers who existed at the tipping point of social convention – some of whom ended up creating brilliant works of art, some not so brilliant, and some helping to invent crazy things like the Internet.

At its height, *Café Magazine* became an international forum connecting people from all walks of life who, in one way or another, were captivated by the plant, the commodity, the drink and the places it was consumed. Over the years the magazine put me in touch with a fascinating group of people who had devoted a good part of their life exploring coffee in its various guises – researchers from coffee trade organisations, small coffee producers, independent café owners, artisan coffee roasters, commodity historians and museum curators. What I found especially intriguing was how many different people, from different countries and different cultures had

11

become engrossed in some aspect of the coffee story – either through occupation, taste or intellect.

Things have changed enormously in England over the years I've been here. It's now more likely to find an excellent cup of coffee on the streets of London where artisan brews have become something of an obsession, than in Paris. England is no longer a nation of tea drinkers (if it ever was) and fine, independent coffeehouse cafés have sprung up in even the smallest towns.

Coffee in the 21st century has become truly globalised in a way that would have been inconceivable when I was a young man. But the story of coffee has always been an epic saga of desire and greed, sagacity and speed, sanctity and sin. It mirrors our world, the creation of which it helped to fuel. It's a story of plants and people – of how people affect plants and how plants affect people. And its effect is remarkable – which is why certain 18th century poets called it the 'Black Apollo'.

INTRODUCTION

THE STORY OF coffee is set in an age when there was a dramatic shift in temporal visions. So the coffeehouse, coffee's unique place of consumption, is an intriguing window through which to view the amazing transformation of life that took place over a very short period of time and helped to construct our contemporary world. But to delve into the story of coffee and cafés in any meaningful way requires a willingness to enter into another domain where we put aside our natural inclination to view history as a linear sequence of events and, instead, weave together narratives from many different strands and many different sources; combining the knowledge of botanist, shaman, merchant, gardener, economist, artist, entrepreneur and consumer.

Unlike a chronicle of nations or societies, the history of a commodity is more open ended. A plant can be looked at organically or commercially. What people do with it and how it comes to affect people's lives is something else again. Therefore, a people's history of a plant must relate to the way it's been used and how it has come to influence social relationships in the human world as well as the botanical one. For coffee is a commodity, like sugar and tobacco, which was the basis of the plantation system, the most brutal exploiter of human labour the world had ever known, and, at the same time, an elixir which fuelled revolutionary thought in Paris, created emporia which momentarily levelled the class divide in London and set the stage for a new economic order in Amsterdam. Yet coffee had only been known in Europe (by the masses, at least) since the 18th century and only used widely as a drink anywhere in the world barely two hundred years before that.

But where did coffee really come from? And how did it get to us? For in the course of a single generation, coffee burst onto the European scene like an Arabian Sirocco. Or did it? And if so, how did that happen in a pre-capitalist world without the trumpeting of the media, as we know it, paving the way for a new and wonderful product?

Certainly, there was a remarkable social restructuring taking place in Europe around the time coffee made its entry. The demise of feudalism, the flowering of mercantilism, the preliminary shoots of an early capitalism – the economic forces of great and dramatic change were tearing Europe asunder and constructing something yet unknown on the ashes of the old. And wherever you looked, there was coffee, the Black Apollo, empowering the new and consigning the moribund to a medieval stupor.

Even more, in the contemporary world where Africa and the Middle East are currently viewed by those in the West as underdeveloped and fanatical, the story of coffee's beginnings had it just the reverse. Neither the commodity of coffee nor the culture of consumption was discovered, invented or recognized by the West until it had been established in the East for over 150 years. Coffee was a drink that promoted diversity and discourse, even if the production of coffee didn't. The most cursory reading of the 16th and 17th century shows us that while European tolerance was in short supply back then, the Ottoman world was a piquant mix of everything on offer.

And so this book is an exploration of how a certain plant became a global commodity, creating fortunes and despair, bringing people together and tearing them apart, playing a starring role in the remarkable awakening of our modern world. The theme is coffee; the venue is the coffeehouse – a place where prince and pauper might meet on equal footing. Where else on earth could we find that?

Photo by Kevin Biderman

❖1❖

Delving into Origins

IT WAS PARIS in the summer of 1714 – a breezy Sunday afternoon. Jean de la Roque hurried down Quai St. Bernard bound for the Jardin des Plants. He'd been invited by Monsieur de Jussien, the head gardener, to witness something that few Europeans had ever seen. Something, indeed, so special that his hands trembled with anticipation and his heart pounded as he strode quickly along the quay.

What could it be that induced such a powerful response in an 18th century Parisian gentleman? The answer might seem a bit prosaic to us looking back more than a quarter of a millennium on. In our mind's eye we see a Paris quite different than the one we know – a Paris with a leg still in the medieval world. Rather than the grand, symmetrical boulevards, this was a city with narrow winding streets and rickety, ancient houses yet to be demolished by great urban planners set loose by future Napoleons. Yet this was a city seething with anticipation. For if one foot was in the old world, the other was firmly planted in the new.

Such a distance tends to blur one's vision, especially when gazing back from an age like ours. Having seen everything there is to see and eaten everything there is eat, our senses have been shattered to a point that there are few surprises left – or so we are led to think.

But back then, two and a half centuries ago, what Jean de la Roque was going to witness was as fantastic to him as the marvels and horrors of bio-technology are to us. Only in one other place, at the famed Hortus Medicus in Amsterdam, had anyone accomplished such a feat – coaxing a coffee tree to bear fruit in European soil.

For Jean de la Roque, seeing this horticultural slight-of-hand was a culmination of an obsession which had plagued him since childhood. He had long been fascinated by the stories of his father who had travelled to Constantinople in 1644 and then to the Levant, bringing back to his home in Marseille not only some of the first coffee ever seen there, but also the enticingly exotic service used in Turkey when entertaining guests – the tiny Fujian cups of ancient China, the little silk napkins embroidered in gold, the delicate silver spoons and the lacquered serving tray.

Coffee was little more than a curiosity when la Roque's father had returned to France, brewed sparingly in drawing rooms of the wealthy or those who had, through travel or trade, contracted the habits of the Levant. But in 1669 something happened which made this substance very much in vogue and launched the epoch of coffee that so fascinated la Roque.

It was in July of that year when the emissaries of Sultan Mohammed IV came to Paris bringing with them sacks upon sacks of a curious bean.

Paris, at the time, was already in the throws of Turkomania as the Empire of the Ottomans pressed ever onward into Europe, till it was knocking at the gates of Vienna itself. Stories of eunuchs dressed in robes of silver and mauve, overseeing their master's erotic needs and courtiers with organs of hearing and speech removed so as to assure their trustworthiness, vied with tales of the Janissaries, the Sultan's elite infantry corps, made up of children torn from their mother's breast as a periodic levy on Christian youth. But it was Constantinople, the ancient seat of Byzantium, which fired the Gallic imagination with shimmering images of silks and spices and all the exotic loot of an empire which stretched from Yemen to Persia to Hungary.

When the Sultan's Ambassador left in May the following year, the coffee habit he introduced into Parisian society had already become the newest fad. People of means were beginning to bring it in from Marseille, or making private arrangements with ship's captains who sailed to the Levant. Yet it wasn't until 1672 that an enterprising Armenian, known simply as 'Pascal', took to selling it publicly, first at the grand fair of Saint Germain and then in a little shop located at the Quai de l'Evole where he sold coffee for two sols, six derniers (or about 2 English pennies) a dish.

La Roque was later to write about a little lame man who, in those years, went through the streets of Paris touting this strange new drink. 'He had a napkin tied about him very neat carrying in one hand a chafing dish made for the purpose, upon which he would set his coffee-pot. In the other hand he carried a kind of fountain full of water, and before him a tin-basket, where he kept all his utensils.'

He was known as 'Candiot'. It seems he just appeared on the scene one day with his companion, a young man named Joseph, who came from the Levant to seek his fortune in Paris.

But that was a generation before. By the time la Roque hurried down the boulevard that summer day in 1714 toward the Jardin des Plants, there was scarcely a town of any size that hadn't one or more coffeehouses. Within a brief period they had sprung up almost magically from one end of the kingdom to another. Coffee had gone from an exotic luxury to a necessary commodity with shiploads of raw beans in rough, muslin sacks coming into harbour almost every day.

Coffee had come of age. What had been small–scale bartering forty years before, had emerged into full-fledged commerce. And the Ottomans, who till now controlled the trade through their Red Sea ports, were quick to realise a good thing when they saw one – as they had been searching for an alternative to the spice monopoly the swaggering Dutch had lifted from them.

'The potentates of Egypt,' la Roque complained, 'have become more difficult in letting that commodity be transported, which has caused a scarcity and raised the price to six and seven haucks per pound.' The hauck was equivalent to about three English pence, and though that seems incredibly small in our inflated age, back then it was certainly enough to make the new entrepreneurs think seriously about alternative sources of supply.

The problem was, however, that alternatives didn't exist to the Red Sea ports – except for one. Which is why the fruiting of that plant la Roque had rushed to witness was so vitally important.

'We went there to see it and observed it a good while with pleasure; it was set in its case and placed in the glass-machine, with the Taper of Peru beside it,' he wrote. 'The Hollander who had that tree under his care came from Marly to the Royal Garden. He told us that there was a great tree of this species in the Hortus Botanicus of Amsterdam whose height was equal to the second story of a house and proportionally as large. That great tree came originally from Arabia, brought from there very young and transported to Java. After some stay, it came at last to Holland where it grew to perfection. The fruit of this same tree, planted in he Garden of Amsterdam, have produced diverse young plants, some of which have born fruit from the age of three years. The shrub sent to our King was of that number, according to the Dutchman.'

It was the scourge of the Ottomans – the Dutch – who first got that bean to grow outside its homeland. Now it had been handed over to the French. What la Roque had witnessed at the Jardin des Plants on that very special Sunday was the Mama tree. It was her progeny that travelled the perilous seas to Dominica. And from there, her grandchildren moved on, jumping from the Caribbean to French Guyana and becoming the founding nurseries of the great coffee empires of South and Central America.

Perhaps this marvel of growing coffee in a European garden can hardly be appreciated now, in our age when human life is nurtured in laboratory test tubes. But it takes more than a green thumb to force a coffee tree to bear fruit outside its native habitat, especially without the technical understanding of soil and nutriments based on sophisticated chemical analysis that we have at our disposal. The critical factors these incredible Dutch gardeners had to contend with in perfecting their Super-tree were, quite simply, astronomical.

To understand what was behind these astounding achievements, however, we need to consider the relationship of humans and plants in the 17th and 18th centuries – a relationship much different than the one we have with vegetables today.

Before the industrial revolution and the dubious marvels of chemistry, plants were the main basis of drugs and tonics which doctors and herbalists prescribed for their patients' health and well-being.

European theologies of the day still accepted the notion that all plants originated in the Garden of Eden and were placed there by God specifically to serve (or tempt) the human race. This belief formed the basis of the ancient theory of 'signatures' which said that each plant gave forth a sign, both in colour and shape, as to its effect. Many herbalists believed that plants could be 'read', and, if interpreted correctly, could be used to cure any known disease.

It was a widely held belief during the Middle Ages that the Garden of Eden had somehow survived the flood, and during the 15th and 16th centuries, the great journeys of exploration kept this item on their agenda along with the search for the Holy Grail and the Fountain of Youth. But by the 17th century, opinion had shifted as the world became more and more charted and pragmatic philosophies of mercantilism became the force to be reckoned with rather than the vague mythologies of the Church which could produce fascinating dreams but very little hard, convertible cash.

The idea of the Garden of Eden, however, persisted even though its current existence was doubted. And, in line with the magnificent arrogance of the time, men began thinking of starting it anew by bringing together all the bits and pieces of creation into one place.

This resurrection of Paradise became a virtual obsession among the new breed of merchant adventurers, perhaps as a rationale for their pillage and looting of the world or, more probably, because they understood that in the new economies being forged, knowledge was power and commodities, wealth.

Most merchant ships, therefore, carried with them a trained botanist whose business it was to discover new vegetation, describe and codify and, hopefully, bring back living specimens for the proliferating botanical gardens which had sprung up in nearly every university town in Britain, Italy and France – though the best gardens, the most brilliant displays of flowering diversity, were owned by the Dutch.

In Leyden, for example, practically every plant known to European naturalists was on display. The garden there was like a botanical encyclopaedia containing examples from the far reaches of the world. Academics, herbalists and medical practitioners awaited each discovery with the anticipation of a physicist learning about another building block of matter. And each new plant would be nurseried and brought to the marvellous Hortus Medicus in Amsterdam, where it would be duly noted in their vast and ever-expanding pharmacopoeia.

The skill of the chief gardeners, like Dutchman Hendrick Gerritsz and Cornelis Vos, in keeping such a monumental collection in bloom, was quite extraordinary. The difficulty, for example, in growing coffee from seed exemplifies the prodigious amount of information necessary in keeping one, let alone thousands of exotic plants, through succeeding generations.

Viability of coffee seeds is comparatively short and germination is a chancy operation at best. Soil warmth is a critical factor, with the optimum temperature hovering at 27.7 degrees Celsius. Propagating the plant through cuttings is equally difficult and requires the maximum of light plus a humidity reading of close to 90%. Rooting can easily take three or four months.

Keeping these things in mind, it's not difficult to understand why the fruition of a coffee tree in a Paris garden might have been such a great event. What is less clear is why it was so important to people who were not in the business of rushing out every time an exotic flower bloomed.

The fascination that Sunday, was, of course, coffee itself – at least for la Roque. His obsession was so great that he ended up writing a book on the subject; the most definitive one to that date.

What interested la Roque was its origins, most likely because of his childhood memories and his father's ritualised use of the ornate paraphernalia he had brought back from Turkey. He had witness coffee emerge from a surreptitious drink, known only to those familiar with the ways of the Levant, to something which burst onto the urban scene, abruptly transforming the course of social life.

Yet the coming of this drink, which Montague said quickened the mind and let the spirit fly, coincided with a period of intense turmoil and change. The noted French historian, Roland Mousnier, even went so far as to call it the 'century of crisis which affected all mankind causing new uncertainties in thought and faith.'

One contemporary observer wrote 'the whole world is shaking'. And, certainly, few people who were around at the time would have denied it. France witnessed well over 1000 revolts during the course of the 17th century and historians have discovered a similar pattern of popular unrest almost anywhere else they cared to look.

Numerous theories have been expounded as to why this century was so extraordinary. Puritans saw the turbulence as a sign from God, warning humankind to mind their wicked ways. Others suggested that malign forces were being influenced by the stars. Modern astronomers now think they might have been right.

Between 1645 and 1715, the skies, according to the records of the time, had a curious absence of sun-spots. And observers from Scandinavia to Scotland noticed another mysterious disappearance – that of the Northern Lights, the Aurora Borealis.

Both these phenomena are indicators of solar energy. The Northern Lights are cause by particles from the sun entering the earth's atmosphere, and sun-spots, themselves, are an indicator of changes in the sun's magnetic fields.

Considering that a decrease of one percent in the total solar radiation can cause a fall of one degree centigrade in mean summer temperature, which in turn restricts the growing season by three to four weeks as well as the maximum altitude at which vegetation will ripen, it's not surprising that a world in which 90% of the total population was dependent on agriculture for food and employment would be thrown seriously out of whack. As a consequence, the population of Europe, between the years 1625 and 1650, fell by twenty percent.

Curiously, this is the very time that coffee first entered Europe. Could it be that la Roque's fascination had something to do with this coincidence? Or perhaps he thought it wasn't a coincidence at all.

In 1714, la Roque stood on a pinnacle. Behind him was a world laid waste by famine, plague and insurrection. Before him was the grand new age of Europe illustrated by the growth of commodity markets and the stock exchange, the empires built on plantation-based trade, and the flowering of the continental cafés.

For the great emerging powers – Holland, England and France – true wealth now came in the form of plants: sugar cane, cotton and tobacco. And, added to the list now was coffee, the new drink that oiled the economic machine and kept it going – the drink that so fascinated the likes of la Roque and seemed to epitomise this new age.

No wonder la Roque tried so hard to delve into its origins, as if its story could shed some light on those extraordinary times. But the history of coffee lay in a past so murky and vague that la Roque, like most of his contemporaries had to resort to third-hand tales in order to trace its way. What he found out was how amazingly little was known – at least in the West. And what was known in the East was shrouded in mystery.

❖2❖

COFFEE'S GARDEN OF EDEN

BEGINNINGS ARE USUALLY where history and myth collide, so the process of seeking out time lines can often be convoluted. But the origin of coffee is even more complicated as there is both the plant and the commodity to consider – or, to be more precise, the various plants and commodities which are loosely bound together in the grab-bag we call 'coffee'.

Ordinarily, when we want to find a beginning, we locate an end point and work our way backwards. For coffee this process depends on when and where we decide to work our way back from. If, for instance, we started our trek homeward along the coffee trail from the Santos region of Brazil in the 1900s, we would be led to a different place (or different places) than if our point of departure was Constantinople in the 1500s.

But if we consider coffee as a commodity, then we also have to determine what form we're talking about. Was coffee used as a food, a medicine, an infusion or a brew? And if the answer is all of the above, then is there a straight line that connects these uses? Was coffee first used as a food, then a medicine, then an infusion, then a brew? Or was it used as all of those at any one time, in many different ways and in many different places?

Coffea Arabica, the type of coffee we in the West

are most familiar with, does have a definite origin, however, and can be traced to the same general area where bones of the earliest hominids were discovered – though, whether Coffea Arabic actually goes back quite as far as Australopithecus afarensis is open to question.

Even if our primeval Lucy and friends hadn't experienced the pleasures of Coffea Arabica in whatever form their collective curiosity allowed, we'd be hard pressed to find a more suitable Garden of Eden than the Harenna Forest in the majestic Bale Mountains, a hundred kilometers or so southeast of Ethiopia's capital city, Addis Ababa. Many eons ago, it seemed to provide the perfect eco-system for both people and plants – and it still does. Though the region is semi-arid, because of the altitude the monsoon winds blowing from the Indian Ocean leave a trail of wetness over the land. The ancient Greeks knew of this forest as did the Romans; so did Solomon and the Queen of Sheba. It is isolated and strikingly beautiful, and the ecology is unique. And it's here in the Harenna forest that botanical historians believe the Coffea arabica plant first grew wild.

In fact, wild coffee plants still populate the Harenna and continue to be harvested by indigenous baboons who seem hopelessly addicted to the bright red berries and their subsequent effect after a brief period of ingestion. And why not? Animals enjoy foods for pleasure as well as sustenance, just like humans. So it's not at all surprising that one of the most enduring legends of coffee's beginnings revolves around the story of a goat.

The tale of Kaldi goes back many centuries and has become incorporated into the folklore of coffee's beginnings in Egypt, Turkey, Syria, Iran, Iraq and Yemen, as well as in its Ethiopian homeland. However, the actual source of this story has never been traced and may, in fact, be one of those parables cobbled together by early European writers that were re-transmitted into Arabic in a curious circularity. Regardless of its origins, each particular country has now put its own take on this charming story, with imagery that connects to their own culture. But essentially the legend is the same: a young shepherd, named Kaldi, is tending his flock in a verdant pasture somewhere in a distant time and distant land where fantasy merges into the ordinary life of shepherds and goats. And it's here that the eponymous Kaldi observes something that will change the lives of millions and will allow this simple shepherd to live forever in story and in verse. For one day, or one night, under a brilliant sky or silvery moon, Kaldi notices something quite strange. A goat which had been quietly munching on some ripe red berries from a nearby shrub has suddenly stood up on its hind legs and started to dance.

In the various illustrations of the Kaldi legend that have been passed down over the years, we usually see the young shepherd dancing blissfully with his flock, holding aloft a sprig of leaves and red berries from a nearby bush. He is often dressed in a tunic, turban, waist sash and breeches – not particularly the clothing an Ethiopian shepherd would have worn in antiquity. But by the time Kaldi became part of coffee mythology, the drink had long been accepted as an Arab invention.

What I think is lovely about the Kaldi story is its universality. A simple shepherd and his goats, in a distant place in a distant time, discover something pleasurable. Man and animal celebrate together. Coffee becomes a gift of nature that is there for everyone, ripe for the picking.

Yet over the years a more secular story of coffee's beginnings slowly emerged through tales of merchants and travellers, readings of ship's logs, factor's reports and especially the writings of those cultural intermediaries who by dint of their special position could function equally well within the Christian and Moslem worlds – namely the Greeks, Armenians, Jews and Banyans.

It is very likely that coffee was used in Ethiopia, its ancestral homeland, for many thousands of years before the invention of the coffee drink. The story of Kaldi and his goats is not so outlandish. People who are dependent on the land for survival have an integral relationship with the earth, its plants and animals – all things that grow. Shepherds, especially, were keen observers regarding what was good to

31

eat and what wasn't. Not everything that animals ate was good for humans, of course. But over the centuries things were tried. Shamans, healers, native herbalists, all had an interest in exotic plants and closely observed their powers as either soporific or stimulant.

The nomadic life was difficult. A shift in weather cycles causing a shortage of resources often forced communities to find new grazing land for their flock. Plants that energized and empowered people to travel long distances without sleep, were highly prized. That the coffee berry was used for these purposes is well known and substantiated both through early travellers' reports and contemporary anthropological research. Even today we find isolated incidents of the coffee plant being used in this manner where the berry – sometimes roasted, sometimes not – is pounded into pulp and mixed with fat into a kind of zingy butter which is spread onto some sort of bread-like substance and then eaten. It might not taste like a good cup of espresso but the effect is the same.

Coffea Arabica existed for thousands of years in the Ethiopian highlands. But coffee as a drink and the coffee culture that surrounds it came from someplace else. And the story of how it got from here to there, how the first emergence of coffee as we have come to know it evolved seemingly out of nowhere, is a fascinating look into a conjunction of possibilities that allow what always existed in one form to become viable in another. In other words, when situations are right, things become manifest. In the case of coffee, several factors came together at a particular time causing a transformation that over the years have taken a curious plant from the isolated wilds and turned it into one of the most successful commodities the world has ever known.

Kaldi and his goats. Anon

❖3❖

THE SUFI CONNECTION

IT WASN'T ONLY la Roque who was captivated by the Black Apollo. Europe's fascination with this new drink sent a number of historians searching for clues as to its origin. The first European to write about coffee was Prosper Alpinus, a famous physician from Padua and a great botanist who accompanied a counsel from the Republic of Venice to Egypt in 1580. Alpinus lived there for several years and wrote a book about Egyptian medicinal plants in which he discussed coffee:

'I have seen at Cairo a tree in the garden of a Turk named Aly Bey, and I have been given the figure of one of its boughs. Tis the same which produces the fruit so common in Egypt which they call "bon" or "ban". There is made with it, among the Arabs and Egyptians, a kind of decoction very much in use and which they drink instead of wine. This drink is called "qahwa" and the fruit comes from Arabia Felix...'

Arabia Felix was the name the Romans gave to the southern end of the Arabian peninsula where dancing waters from silvery streams rushed down pristine mountains into rich, fertile valleys below.

Fantastic? Perhaps to us, but not to Alexander-the-Great whose dream was to retire there. That land, known now as Yemen, was as distant as the moon to Europeans of the day. Hardly anyone travelled there.

And when they did, it was with wonder and awe that they would describe it.

Yemen was at the far reaches of the Ottoman Empire – traversed by only the bravest European merchant adventurers. Travel writers then were few and far between. And of those daring explorers who did wander into the unknown, certainly none could compare with the Englishman, George Sandys, who went simply out of curiosity.

Departing Venice in 1610, he voyaged through the Turkish dominions for several years like a wayward Odysseus, several times fleeing from pirates and finding himself caught up in strange caravans. Once, journeying through the hot desert to the Holy Lands, he joined a group of elderly Jewish women who 'at the extremity of their age were undertaking so wearisome a journey only to die at Jerusalem: bearing along with them the bones of their parents, husbands, children and kinfolk.'

Sandys, unlike the merchants he travelled with, was fortunately a keen observer of daily life. Writing of Turkish drinking habits, he said, 'Although they be destitute of taverns, they have their coffa-houses, which something resemble them. They sit there chatting most of the day and sip a drink called "coffa" in little china dishes as hot as they can suffer it: black as soot, and tasting not much unlike it.' (As an afterthought, perhaps as an explanation for this curious state of affairs, he added, 'Many of the coffa-men keep beautiful boys who serve to procure them customers.')

But it wasn't until many years later that a European travel writer, named Niebuhr, reached Yemen, itself. 'On the first day of our journey,' wrote Niebuhr, 'we rested in a coffeehouse situated near a village. "Mokeya" is the name give by Arabs to such places which stand in the open country and are intended, like our inns, for the accommodation of travellers. They are mere huts and are scarcely furnished with a "serir" or long seat of straw ropes; nor do they afford any refreshment but "kischer," a hot infusion of coffee beans. This drink is served out of coarse earthen cups; but persons of distinction always carry porcelain cups in their baggage. The master of the coffeehouse lives commonly in some neighbouring village whence he comes every day to wait for passengers...'

This was a far cry from the opulent rooms bedecked in silks and velvet that came to be the pride of cities like Baghdad, Damascus and Istanbul. On the other hand, the village in which Niebuhr found himself was only a short distance from the hills in which coffee was grown and but a few days journey from the harbour of Mocha, where this commodity was exported.

By the time Niebuhr came along, coffee was already well known in Europe and the mokeya had been a part of Yemeni life for hundreds of years. Still, he was one of the first Europeans to describe it; an indication of how distant and strange Yemen was even in the mid-18th century. So it's hardly surprising that historians like la Roque, let alone naturalists like Alpinus, could find little to say about coffee's origins.

When Prosper Alpinus went to Egypt, coffee had been used there for more than a half century. In 1510 there was not a single coffeehouse in Cairo. But just twenty years later, there were multitudes, as witnessed by a Turkish writer who stayed there for a while and noted 'the concentration of coffee-houses at every step. Early rising worshippers and pious men, get up and go there, drink a cup of coffee adding life to their life. They feel, in a way, the slight exhilaration strengthens them for their religious observance and worship.' Cairo, however, produced no coffee and Alpinus could trace this bean no further than his vague reference to Arabia Felix. But Philippe Sylvestre Dufour, who wrote a small book published in 1685 with the intriguing title – *Traitez Nouveux et Curieux Du Café, du Thé et du Chocolate* – thought he could fix the origin in Persia.

'The first that makes mention of the property of this bean, under the name of "bunchum" in the 9th century was Zachary Mohomet Rases, commonly called Rhasio, a very famous Arab physician,' Dufour wrote. He then set forth the thesis that coffee, in fact, came from Persia and had been known in that part of the world for nearly a millennium.

Dufour was wrong. But his disastrous error – which led writers astray for generations – gives us a special insight into the historical process and emphasises why following the path of anything that crosses cultural and linguistic divides is so incredibly tricky. There is a strange rule of history which allows any bit of information that goes unchallenged to pass from generation to generation as if age alone bestows it with authority. Believability becomes a question of reference.

The problem was one of language and the fact that European Arabists were something like Latin scholars. They had an excellent classical background, but most of them knew nothing of the living language, nor could they pick up on the multitude of meanings and nuances in such a rich and metaphorical tongue.

In Arabic, the word 'El Ajem' means 'foreign'. Depending on where it is spoken, the word can refer to different lands. In the northern parts of the Arabian peninsula, it can mean Persia. But in the south, the term is used in reference to the people of the opposite coast – specifically, Sudan and Ethiopia.

Similarly the Arabic words 'qahwa' which has come to mean 'coffee', and 'bun' or 'bunchum', which now is used as a term for 'coffee bean', had a multitude of references depending on where or when it was written or spoken.

'Qahwa' is a general term which in ancient times meant 'wine', but changed in meaning as the dictates of the Moslem religion led to prohibition of alcoholic drinks. It came to mean a 'brew' or 'infusion' without a substance being specified. It could mean 'coffee'. But, equally, it could mean an infusion from a plant called 'qat' which was used in the south long before coffee was known.

These variations in meaning caused no end of problems for the European writers who dared to use the fragments of Arab manuscripts that came their way which seemed to promise an authoritative clue to coffee's origin. But definition of specific words was only part of the quandary. The major stumbling block had to do with the differing notions of history, itself.

By the time la Roque had come along, history in the West was already a straightforward, pragmatic venture controlled, in the main, by secularists. Writers, of course, had their benefactors and it was still very much the vogue to start one's book with a lengthy and unctuous benediction directed toward their patron of the day.

But in the Moslem world there was no distinction between secular and religious. Cause and effect were ever entwined with the dictates of the Koran. And the Arabic language seemed to delight in flowing obliquely, in tangents, like their intricate mosaic tiles.

The origin of things had a different meaning in the East than in the West. For starters, everything came from God. So history was more of a parable, which incorporated moral issues and hints of Grand Design, within its context.

Since history and poetry were almost interchangeable in the Arab world, translation from one language to another had little chance of success if it was done with a literal bent. Success lay in cracking the metaphor.

So what were these stories which the Arab world passed on to explain the origin of coffee? Not surprisingly, they had to do with mystics. There were many variations of these epic tales, which appealed more to the imagination than to the intellect, but they all seemed to run along a common line: a Sufi sheikh saves his followers from a deadly plague or famine by feeding them coffee berries which an apparition leads him to discover in the foothills near the Yemeni seacoast.

The interesting part of these stories is that they assume coffee grew wild in the vicinity of Mocha, which it very well might have done by mid-thirteenth century, when the events in these tales were to have taken place. They also imply that prior to this time the drink was unknown – at least in Arabia. Lastly, they link the origin of coffee consumption to the Sufi order within Islam – a fact substantiated by other historical documentation. But if coffee wasn't sent to the Arabs by a messenger of God, the question still remained: where did they get it from?

It's not difficult to understand how the coffee plant could have made the short jump across the Red Sea from Ethiopia to Yemen. But that doesn't help us solve the mystery of why coffee became a drink, or how, in a few short years, it rose from obscurity to become a commodity of enormous importance. To follow what happened, though, we need a little background:

At the end of the 15th century, the Arab world was undergoing a major retreat from its points of expansion. The Christian reconquest of Spain was nearly complete and, in the east, the Egyptian Caliphate, having become hopelessly corrupt, was under threat by the Ottoman Turks. Even worse, the Portuguese who had founded new sea routes to India, now were able to bypass the Red Sea ports, thus squeezing the Islamic merchants out of the lucrative pepper trade. And the great caravans loaded down with spices from the East, faded silently into the rippling desert heat, now little more than a mirage. For many Arab writers, this time was seen as a period of decline and despair – summed up in the words of a contemporary poet:

'...for that I live in an age become exceedingly strange Cruel and terrible, wherein we need Most urgently a statement of our faith...'

A deep sense of malaise prevailed in the lands of the crescent moon. And there were those who began searching for something to fill the spiritual and economic void, the great chasm in the heart of Islam.

It was within this context that Sufism, a mystic order that sought to look beyond the material world, took root amongst the masses who were beginning to see themselves marching down the long, dusty

41

road to oblivion. In the final decades of the 15th century the Sufi ranks swelled as thousands of artisans, labourers and students dug their way from the debris of the collapsing social edifice to follow their local saint, hoping to find some illumination to brighten up the shadows of their bleak existence.

Like many leaders of mass religious movements which are suddenly besieged with such desperate converts, more than a few Sufi sheikhs were quick to see the advantage in having gained so loyal and obedient a flock. Naturally, it wasn't long before Sufism became a prime target of attack from established secular and religious leaders who saw this pesky, but rather docile sect, become, in their eyes at least, a full-fledged political threat.

However, Sufism was neither a strictly hierarchical order, nor was it monastic. In fact, each adherent was encouraged to seek his own path of enlightenment. The Sufi who set forth to find God called himself a 'traveller' and he advanced by slow stages toward the goal of union with the great universe of the spirit – something like the quest of the gurus in the 1960's generation who exhorted their followers to 'turn on, tune in and drop out.' Like then, the dissatisfaction with the trappings of secular wealth and the perceived hypocrisy of the established order led to massive experimentation with devices which might transport those many unhappy souls to another realm, where the burdens of everyday life could be left behind and spirits might soar.

Of course, for a devout Muslim, the Koran was quite specific about which substances could or could not be taken into the body to help the spirit gain flight. Wine, or any similar beverage, was definitely out. So the ingredient that other cultures and religions had found the quickest way to nirvana, namely alcohol, was denied them.

On the other hand, Sufism was not the individual, quiet contemplation of a Christian monk floating off in an alcoholic haze. Indeed, it was very social and far from quiet. If the way to God was through denial of self, it was better to do it with such fervour that each spirit would leap from the body and come together in the oneness of the divine. Thus a typical Sufi gathering was characterized by a frenzy of activity which gave rise to the whirlwind images related by astounded European explorers after witnessing the dancing dervishes of the Sufi sects whose chanting gyrations could easily go on throughout the night.

Parties like that don't go very far without a stimulus. So the need for an amphetamine-like substance existed. And in the same general location there was a plant which provided such a drug. The only thing necessary was to put the two together.

Ibriq

❖4❖

EGYPTIAN CHRYSALIS

HAVING BEEN ESTABLISHED in the Sufi community of Yemen, the coffee trail quite naturally followed the trade routes travelled by a steady stream of merchants, buyers and sellers, many of whom were Sufis already addicted to the caffeinated prowess the roasted bean provided.

By the last decade of the 15th century there were dedicated coffee stops along these well-trod paths. Known as Kaveh Kanes, they were originally places where wandering Sufis could practice their rituals.

The spread of coffee along the ancient arteries of the Levant, stretching from Mecca to Aleppo and then on to Baghdad and Mosul to the east and Alexandria and Cairo to the west, was quick indeed. Initially connected to the Sufi dakhrs that had taken up the ritual use of coffee as practiced in Yemen, it wasn't long until a nascent coffee culture began to take root in cities and towns throughout the Middle East.

It was Cairo, at the dawning of the 16th century, where we have one of the first detailed descriptions of how this new coffee culture was developing. A Sufi theological complex, located in the Yemeni district of the city, served it up at their religious gatherings. The Arab historian Ibn 'Abd al-Ghaffar gives us an indication of the ritual use of coffee in these Sufi ceremonials:

'They drank it every Monday and Friday eve, putting it in a large vessel made of red clay. Their leader ladled it out with a small dipper and gave it to them to drink, passing it to the right, while they recited [their blessings]...'

It wasn't long before coffee started to appear on the streets as word got around of its potency; and it quickly emerged as a drink in its own right – not only as a promised pathway to God. It may have tasted bitter, but ordinary people in Cairo loved it (though it must be said that sweeteners and other condiments were soon added). Coffee made them feel good – bright and alert. It cleared their heads. They drank it hot from small porcelain cups, as hot as they could stand it.

A curiosity of the Arab world was that, unlike in Europe, there had never been a culture of drinking halls or restaurants. People entertained at home, which meant that, except for the market and the mosque, society was housebound. Taverns did exist but not for proper Muslims. So the development of an alternative social meeting place, not connected to the mosque and not tainted with the scent of the profane, was something that urbane Arabs craved.

But before coffee drinking could become universally approved in the Muslim world, something else had to be considered. Coffee drinking as part of Sufi ritual ceremonies, where it was used rather like wine in Christendom, was one thing. Drinking it for pleasure was quite another. Was it legal beyond religious ritual? In some communities it was, in others a legal judgement from the leading mullahs would be issued and coffee as a popular drink would be forbidden – at least for a while. As it happened, unsurprisingly, the test came in the town that gave birth to the religion of Mohammed.

In 1511 the governor of Mecca – by all accounts a particularly officious bureaucrat – was leaving the mosque one evening after prayers and was offended by a boisterous group loitering outside who were drinking some unknown substance. He first thought they were imbibing wine, which was strictly forbidden; as it turned out they were only drinking coffee. But since this group who were balancing small white cups in their hands seemed talkative, loud, and exuberant, the governor concluded that the drink in those little porcelain cups, midnight black, must lead men to wantonness. As a faithful guardian of public morality, he was determined to suppress it. A council of religious scholars was duly convened and after discussing the disturbance witnessed that evening, it was decided such gatherings should be forbidden, along with the substance that was deemed to have caused this unseemly behaviour – coffee.

As long as coffee remained a ceremonial beverage, there wasn't a problem with its legality. It was only when coffee became a popular drink beyond the reach of the mosque that it was looked upon by those in power as a suspect commodity. The real fear, of course, wasn't coffee; it had to do with what was happening at those clandestine nocturnal gatherings where coffee was being drunk. But attempts to ban coffee drinking were never successful. The genie – in this case the bean – was already out of the bottle and it wouldn't be possible for anyone, no matter what their standing, to ever force it back in.

The triumph of pomposity in Mecca in 1511 was short-lived, for the Caliphate at Cairo disapproved of this zealous administrator and ordered the edict revoked. But the Mamluk dynasty, the sultanates that had ruled Egypt for over two hundred years, was reaching its conclusion as well. In 1517 Cairo fell to the Ottomans. By the end of the decade much of the Middle East and a good part of North Africa was in the hands of the Turks. And in the Ottoman world a phenomenon was brewing that catapulted coffee into a new dimension and, almost overnight, would forever transform the landscape of urban culture.

Turkish café, Lithograph. Bibl. des Arts décoratifs, Paris

❖ 5 ❖

THE OTTOMAN LAUNCH PAD

COFFEE AND COFFEEHOUSES were well established in the Levant before coming to Istanbul. Spreading north from Egypt up through Syria, by the mid-16th century they had become the most important institutions of social intercourse. Unlike the degenerate pits described by some writers, the coffeehouses in cosmopolitan centres of the Levant, like Damascus, were luxurious – consciously modelled on the Arabic vision of Paradise.

Many of them were situated by parks and rivers and had a relaxing, garden-like atmosphere. Inside, there were profusions of plants and ornate fountains. Customers would sit on the benches and divans that lined the walls. Outside, there were seats for those who wanted to drink in the cool of the breeze and, like habitués of the modern metropolitan café, watch the passers-by.

Just as it had in Arabia, so the growth of the coffee habit in Turkey stirred a strong reaction at first. In the early 17th century, certain elements within the religious community became concerned about the 'hypocritical mystics' congregating along with the Imams, 'who were in danger of becoming coffeehouse addicts.' Again, fatwas were imposed, declaring coffee unfit for Muslims to drink. In response, coffeehouses were, for a time, closed down. However, a form of speakeasies took their place. Termed 'armpit' coffeehouses, these were to be found in blind alleys and at the back of certain shops. Bribes, judiciously passed to the chiefs of police, ensured that customers continued to enjoy the pleasures of their drink unhindered.

Nothing, it seemed, could inhibit the Turkish citizenry's quest for this potent stimulant. The edicts of the mullahs were rescinded and the prohibition ceased – proving once again, if proof be needed, that it takes more than pious dictates to stop a good idea, especially one that is physically addictive.

An account of how coffee first entered the portals of the Grand Signor is given by the 17th century writer, Ibrahim Pecevi. Born in what is now southern Hungary, he was a forward-looking historian who tried to integrate Islamic ideas and contemporary European thought. Fascinated by the coffeehouse as a popular school of arts and culture, Pecevi tried to find out how these drinking establishments first came to Istanbul. He discovered that several traders, Hakem, from Aleppo, and Shems, from Damascus, had opened the first coffee shops at Takht ul-Kale, a district in Istanbul just north of the kan, the great covered market, and near to the bustling harbour. There, he said:

'Certain lovers of pleasure and more especially certain wits of the literary classes, would gather and hold sessions – twenty or thirty men in each coffee shop. Some would read out books and elegant compositions and some would settle down to backgammon and chess. Others used to bring newly composed lyrics and discuss the arts.'

The two coffeehouses had quickly gained an enormous following and soon 'there was not a seat to be had or even standing room!' Clearly fascinated by such a phenomenal success story, Pecevi goes on to tell how, overnight, the coffeehouse became an established fixture within the capital: 'Apart from those who held high office, even the notables could not help coming.' Unfortunately, Pecevi says nothing more about the founders of the coffeehouses. Nor does he pursue the curiosity that they existed simultaneously in the same part of town; possibly across from one another. We are left to contemplate an enigma in the early life of coffee.

By 1560 there were at least 50 coffeehouses in Istanbul; by 1570 there were over 600. Smaller neighbourhoods had their own coffee shops, though not as grand as the ones in the major business areas. People began to locate themselves by describing where they lived in relation to the nearest coffeehouse. So what did these new coffeehouses provide that was different? And how did they help establish coffee as a commodity worthy of international interest?

Certainly the social structure of the Ottomans was distinct from the European countries that first took up coffee in the late 17th century. The Muslim world had its hierarchies, of course, but not the same sort of class structure based on noble birth found in Europe. For a citizen of Istanbul it was possible to rise to any station without having a pedigree. Thus the 'social levelling' factor of the coffeehouse did not have the same connotations that it would in Europe. But the travellers who brought back reports to France, England, Italy, and the Germanies would emphasise the point that the Ottoman coffeehouse served all sorts of people who gathered there for common pleasure and shared interests. And these same travellers were quick to see that, unlike alcohol, the coffee served actually promoted the very things that gin, wine, and beer seemed to suppress—quickness of wit and gentleness of manner.

Coffee had rapidly become an integral part of the Ottoman culture and has survived as such to this day. It is said that in Turkey some men still choose their wives by, among other things, how well they use the ibriq. And fortunes are told not by sifting through the dregs of tea, but from the leftover grounds in the coffee cup. More importantly perhaps, it was Turkey that became the launching point for coffee's entry into Europe.

The huge economic cauldron of the Ottoman Empire was spilling over into the Germanic states, and this process was further expedited by two groups of people whose dispersal throughout both Europe and the Middle East gave them a special relationship with both the Christian and Muslim worlds: the Jews and the Armenians (often referred to as 'Greeks'). They were the intermediaries who moved freely through the selective barriers that divided those vast empires. And, when the time was right to spread the word about the coming of coffee, they would be the chosen ones.

Word of the new phenomenon of coffee cafés was slow to filter back to Europe, but some travellers did write about this curious trend. One of the more interesting of these reports was by Pedro Teixeira, who came from a family of Marranos, the clandestine Jews forced to convert to Christianity during the Spanish Inquisition. Teixeira travelled the world between 1586 and 1605, visiting Cuba, Mexico, California, the Philippines, Sumatra, Malacca, Goa, and finally the Middle East where he observed with fascination the growing importance of the coffeehouse and coffee culture. He wrote:

'Among other public buildings there is also a coffeehouse. In these houses, all meet who want to drink it, noblemen as well as commoners. As they sit together they are served this drink very hot in small porcelain cups. Everyone takes a cup in his hand, blows a little and then sips from it. The drink is black and has little taste and although some good qualities are attributed to it, none are known for certain. However, it is the custom to meet here and chat and they derive much enjoyment from it.

In order to attract more customers, handsome boys who are richly dressed are chosen to serve the coffee and receive the money, accompanied by music and other entertainments. During the summer these houses are frequented mainly at night and in the winter during the day. The great coffeehouse is situated near the river, which can be overlooked from windows and galleries and makes it a very pleasant place to relax. There are several such houses in the town and many others in all Turkish lands and in Persia there are coffeehouses very notable for their structure and furnishings and decorated with many lamps as they are busiest at night but they are also well attended during the day.'

The real drawback in the minds of the travellers who visited these establishments was the drink itself. Coffee to their palate was a bitter brew that tasted even worse than the stuff that was served up in Arabia. At least there the beans were sometimes fresh, unlike Istanbul where they were stored in leather sacks and often subject to mildew. But once the squeamishness of European taste buds was recognized, visitors from those 'pagan' lands were offered sugar – even though a spoonful of sugar in those days was probably more expensive than the coffee in the cup they were sweetening.

If Yemen saw the germination of the coffee trade and the Egyptian caliphate its nurture, Ottoman Istanbul was coffee's proving ground as a world-class commodity. And the institution that provided the engine for this to happen was the metropolitan coffeehouse. Although by the end of the 16th century coffeehouses existed in most of the important urban centres of Egypt and Arabia, what made Istanbul different – and why it is so important in the story of how coffee gained a global identity – was that it didn't simply adopt the coffeehouse culture of Arabia. In Istanbul, coffee and the public space where it was consumed became an obsession, transforming the metropolitan landscape and creating a new, secular and outward-looking popular culture that was exciting, economically rewarding, and highly marketable to the West.

There are certain times and circumstances that allow things to happen as if they were always meant to be, causing us to wonder why it took so long. But it takes more than fertile soil for flowers to spread; it also takes the buzzing of bees and their ability to pollinate plants. In coffee's case, the bees were people and the gardens that provided the pollen were the coffeehouses.

The new coffeehouses that had arrived in the late 16th century were a key part of the new model city that was taking shape. Civil and secular society had come of age and needed a place to congregate. Up till then there were three gathering points: the mosque, the market, and the bathhouse. For non-Muslims there were taverns, of course. But they were not in favour and served only a small portion of the city's populace. (They would have been nailed shut except for the fact that the wine trade provided a very large tax bounty that the government was loath to give up.) The coffeehouse offered a new meeting place for a new society.

By the mid-17th century the consumption of coffee in Turkey had become an economic force to be reckoned with. It was soon so prevalent a drink that the Grand Viziers used part of their fortunes to build ornate coffeehouses, rent them out, and watch their earnings soar. Women used the withholding of coffee by their husbands as a legal excuse to sue for divorce. And wealthy agas, when they were feeling especially benevolent, would order that a pot of coffee be brewed to fill up the begging bowls in the trembling hands of the caffeine-starved dervishes who waited, restlessly, outside their houses.

As the 17th century progressed, Istanbul became a centre of the most exciting economy in the world, since a good part of the extraordinary wealth from the Ottoman Empire was deposited there. Personal incomes were on the rise with the consequence that people's purchasing power was at an all-time high. The port of Istanbul held a mountain of goods imported from all around the world, and freighters bound for foreign shores waited in turn to fill their holds with everything from luscious silks to fragrant spices and foul-smelling leathers.

Istanbul itself had changed remarkably over the course of several decades. It had spread beyond the ancient walls and expanded into a metropolis that was one of the largest urban conglomerations in the world. And now that its citizens had expendable incomes, they wanted places to buy things and they wanted new things to buy. In response, the streets of Istanbul became crowded with shops that sold everything you could think of. For the first time, people stopped baking their own bread and pastries and bought them instead at a store. Istanbul, unlike the dreary cities of Europe, had become a template for modernism. When Europe woke from its medieval lethargy, it was Ottoman fashions – including their taste for coffee – that would catch the collective imagination.

The Ottoman world was at the pinnacle of its power, symbolized in a sense by its ability to control the lucrative coffee trade. But fresh winds were blowing from the west and the sails of ships from two mighty concerns had been unfurled. In the following decades the Dutch Verenigde Oostindische Compagnie (the VOC) and the English East India Company would play a role in the life of coffee that not only broke the Ottoman monopoly but also carried the coffee plant to the four corners of the world, producing so many beans for so many markets that by the next century the port of Mocha would be essentially moribund.

❖6❖
THE DISCOVERY OF COFFEE BY THE EAST INDIA COMPANY

IN THE YEARS between coffee's first use in the Sufi dhikrs and the rise of the Ottoman coffeehouse in Istanbul, Yemen had grown fat on the coffee bean. Not only had her key port of Mocha thrived as the demand for coffee grew exponentially in the early 17th century, but in the verdant hills to the east an extraordinary change had come about. Over the decades the mountainous terrain had been transformed. Where once there had been tiny villages and subsistence farms, a new crop had taken over, colonising the land for many miles around. The ancient paths to the port cities that once had seen the occasional mule train plodding along were now well-trodden roads alive with a constant flow of traffic. And where before only the intrepid adventurer would have been seen in those sparsely populated mountain villages, now men flocked from Egypt, Syria, Turkey, and Persia – men with wads of money in their pouches bidding for the rights to participate in one of the greatest commodity trades the world had ever known. These were the coffee merchants who had come great distances to Yemen's sacred coffee mountains, which for the past century had been and for several decades yet would continue to be the only source for the product so keenly desired throughout the lands controlled by the Ottomans and beyond.

The port of Mocha, the major harbour of the Yemeni coffee trade, was still filled with ships awaiting cargo for transport to key entry points of the intricate supply chain that criss-crossed the east. But now, instead of spices, it was sacks of coffee beans that were loaded into holds. Of these sacks, the vast majority were headed for the great warehouses of Cairo and Alexandria, whence they would be again trans-shipped by boat or camel train to the far reaches of the Empire where they would be stored in cities and towns to supply the local trade.

Coffee had become gold. In fact, when money was in short supply people sometimes used coffee beans as a medium of exchange instead of coins. The Ottoman state understood fully the importance of protecting the goose that was laying these cherry-like eggs and went to great lengths to defend their monopoly by making the coffee mountain as secure as 17th century technology would allow.

Coffee shrubs were closely guarded and beans were processed prior to export so they could not be germinated by foreign gardeners. But Yemen was a big country and plants are difficult to control when it comes to propagation. Besides, the coffee plant did already exist in other places – in East Africa, of course, and in India where coffee had been grown from very early days, though never for anything more than a local market.

On the evening of April 7, 1609 one of the first British ships ever to visit Yemen came to anchor outside the port of Aden. Of course the English had heard stories of this great port, thick with freighters and junks which tramped the coasts of India bringing exotic goods from the East to be exchanged for European commodities like woollens, leathers, tin and iron, brought down from Suez by ship or caravan. But, to the surprise of the men aboard the Ascension, the historic harbour of Aden was curiously deserted, except for a few Gujarati vessels; and the city, itself, what they could see of it, seemed run-down and seedy as if the businessmen had all gone elsewhere and the place had been left to rot.

Even so, the ship's officers were warmly welcomed by the Governor of Aden, a Greek renegade who administered the city for the Turks. They were entertained with 'tabour and pipe', given a robe of honour and offered splendid accommodation in which to rest. Assured by the Governor that their goods would find a quick and ready sale, they went to sleep that night secure in the thought that a year of tribulation, fighting the perils of the seas, would at last be rewarded.

The following day, the ship's cargo of cloth and metal was purchased for the Pasha and brought to shore accompanied by several of the ship's merchant representatives, two men named Jourdain and Revett, who were sent to settle the accounts.

Once ashore, however, the Governor, intent on gaining whatever profit he could from these Christian heathens, declared an enormous customs duty on all goods landed, whether sold or not. Jourdain, the chief factor, refused to accept such outrageous extortion. But the Governor stood fast. If the factors wished to appeal, he said, they could take their claim up personally with the Pasha. That would mean, of course, travelling overland to San'a – a treacherous journey of several weeks which would probably end in disaster.

Foolhardy stubbornness was a trait which marked these merchant buccaneers. So, as their ship set sail for Mocha to see about picking up some indigo which was said to have recently arrived, Jourdain and Revett set out on camel to journey several hundred miles through mountainous terrain bound for the centre of Ottoman rule in Yemen, the town of San'a.

Jourdain wrote in his journal that they left on the 26th of May in the company of 'two renegades, our drogamon, one Italian and another a Frenchman.' They travelled often at night, sometimes till three in the morning, passing 'high mountains full of stones and very dangerous for thieves.'

On the 3rd of June they reached the city of Hippa, a garrison town where they rested in a caravansary. 'The very fertile nature of the land surrounding the city yields fruit every three months,' wrote Jourdain. He also spoke of the kindness of the Governor there who sent a goat for Jourdain and his men to eat. They stayed two days, in the evening going to the hot house to bathe while the Governor's man kept them company.

Then, on June 5th, they left Hippa early in the morning to cross the great mountain which rose ominously in their path. 'From this mountain,' wrote Jourdain, clearly enraptured by the magnificence of the sight, 'runs many rivers that water Arabia; and from its soil springs many grains and fruit. The way is paved so five men may go abreast all the way up.'

Such a large highway in the middle of nowhere? It seemed incredible. What was the need? On top of the hill were two strong castles by means of which the Turks commanded the passage. Nearby was a town where Jourdain and his companions stopped. Here atop the great mountain, they were astonished to find a town buzzing with activity. The marketplace was thick with merchants and traders – Arabs, Indians, Persians – haggling in a babble of exotic tongues. But what drew them to this distant spot?

Anxious to find out about the nature of this thriving commerce, Jourdain – adept in the art of commercial espionage – quickly located some likely informants and exchanged a few worthless goods for information. He was told that the mountain was named Nasmarde and that it was a very special place. For on this mountain grew most of the qahwa (which Jourdain heard as 'cohoo') that was shipped throughout all the lands controlled by the Turks and to the far reaches of the Indies.

What Jourdain and Revett had stumbled upon that day was Yemen's coffee mountain – the produce of which, by then, had become more valuable than gold (at least for those who had been seduced by this exotic substance). Though coffee had yet to make its entry into Europe, by 1610, the year these stalwarts from the East India Company arrived, it had become one of the most important commodities in the Turkish Empire.

Let us stop a moment and consider this remarkable intersection where two worlds crossed, by chance, like an apparition meeting up with its destiny on a verdant mountain top. Two English merchant adventurers, trekking through an unknown wilderness, as strange and forbidding as being lost in the pages of Arabian Nights, suddenly came face-to-face with the commodity that several generations hence would sweep through their homeland like an economic mistral, changing the face of society and making vast fortunes for merchants very similar to themselves. However they could hardly see across that chasm of time which separated knowledge from fantasy, dreams from truth, or a handful of beans from a silver ingot. For there was still a quarter century yet to go before a dish of coffee would be sold on English soil.

Jourdain and Revett, though, were clear that they had found out something quite significant. These two young factors, after all, were trained and resourceful agents of an organisation soon to become an economic power as great, in relationship to its world, as any multinational concern we know today; and they duly noted the information they had pried from their straightforward hosts, eventually passing it on to their home office which filed it away with all the other mass of records which accumulated in vast piles in musty rooms, sifted through slowly by 17th century bureaucrats.

Leaving Nasmarde, Jourdain and Revett continued on to San'a, accomplishing their mission (the Pasha was most understanding and agreed immediately to full recompense) and after a few other adventures (like spending the night with a blind, Portuguese warlock), they made their way to Mocha, where they finally met up with their ship.

Unlike Aden, the two factors found Mocha 'very populous' with merchants from many cities of Islam and the Indies. Thirty-five sailing ships from Ormus, Dieu, Chaulel, Tatta, Daman and Sinda, crowded into the harbour together with freighters from Suez. They came there, Jourdain wrote, because of the 'staple'. One merchandise now reigned supreme and had brought life back to this ancient city. It was coffee, the very commodity they had seen just days ago on Nasmarde, now stacked neatly in mountainous piles of sacks which towered over the wharf.

Were Jourdain and Revett the first Englishmen to see a coffee plant? Certainly they were among the first to intimately understand its economic importance, if not for the European market then as a vital commodity of exchange in the Middle East. Forty years before the English or Dutch merchants started bringing coffee into Europe, they were well aware of its value in the Middle East and India. They knew where it was grown, what price it brought and its port of origin. The only thing they didn't know was why people wanted it so much. And until they knew that, it wasn't worth bringing back home.

However, that didn't stop British merchants from using it in the form of commodity exchange, which the English East India Company started doing a few years later – especially between their factories in Surat (on the Gurjarat coast) and Jask (the Indian Ocean port for Persia.) Well before it ever reached the Thames Estuary, English shippers had experience in how to buy and store the stuff.

Why didn't some clever entrepreneur jump the gun and take advantage of this lengthy gap in the marketplace? One reason is that even when a market exists for a commodity somewhere, there is no guarantee it exists someplace else. The East India Company was well aware of this. Out of the hundreds of condiments and spices used in India, only a dozen or so 'sold' well in European markets. The reverse was also true. Sage, for instance, which was used as a tea in England during the 17th century, couldn't be given away in Asia. They just didn't like the flavour.

The idea behind trans-shipping, in fact, was knowing where something was wanted and where it wasn't. English iron could be traded for coffee in Mocha which then could be shipped to Surat and traded for spice which then could be taken to Jask and traded for Persian carpets. Theoretically, in each case a profit was made even if money never changed hands. The final exchange, hopefully, gave the merchants a cargo that would sell well in England, the value being that much greater because of all the previous transactions.

In fact, coffee was to become an item of desire in Europe – far beyond anyone's expectations. But what kind of imagination would it have taken to understand that Europe was ready for a long drink of Arabica? And, even if that could be imagined by some prescient merchant, how could he have put it into motion? You don't just take an unknown commodity and dump it in the marketplace. Either the demand is there or you have to know how to create it. Back then there weren't any advertisers to beat the drums over the airwaves. Building a market was a slow, laborious task. If the demand for a particular commodity was there, someone might be able to fill it. But it had to be economically worthwhile before a merchant invested a goodly sum to ship a product halfway round the world. The polished techniques of creating desire as an integral part of merchandising commodities came much later in the history of capitalism.

❖ 7 ❖

COFFEE'S ENTRY INTO EUROPE

BY THE 17TH century global trade relations had become very complex and sophisticated. We in the West naturally tend to see these relationships from our own limited perspective. But the system of entrepôts, or foreign trading stations where goods could be warehoused for future transhipment, wasn't only a feature of European mercantilism – Western settlements in India, Persia, Egypt and Turkey were mirrored by Eastern outposts, small as they might have been, in places like Venice, Marseille, London and Amsterdam – indeed in all the major ports that were involved in global exchange.

These communities were porous, fluid and sometimes nearly invisible but like their counterparts in Constantinople, Alexandria and Surat, the people who staffed these 'colonies' (which might have been as tiny as a room in a house) would have maintained their cultural and culinary routines as best they could. By the 17th century, coffee certainly would have been one of those items brought, delivered or sought by those Eastern merchants, traders or embassy staff stationed in Europe who had consumed the drink on a regular basis back home.

Intriguingly, coffee was listed as a commodity that was offloaded in the port of Amsterdam well before there was a popular market for it. Who was this coffee intended for? Was it sold to foreign residents or simply warehoused for trans-shipment? No one knows for sure. But on the Mediterranean, at ports like Venice, Livorno or Marseille, where there had long been direct relations with the people of North Africa and the Levant, it's inconceivable that there wasn't a community, however small, who were roasting and brewing coffee for themselves as well as introducing this exotic drink to invited guests.

Even though coffee was still relatively unknown in northern Europe, by the early 1600s it had penetrated into the highest echelons of society. We know from contemporary writers like la Roque how intrigued visitors were by the coffee service on display at his father's house in Marseille. We also know how much Parisian society was influenced by the retinue that accompanied the Ottoman delegation taking up residence there.

In England, similar cultural interchange took place in academic centres such as Oxford where coffee was used very early on by scholars who had brought back items of curiosity from Cairo or Constantinople; while in London William Harvey and Francis Bacon, both attached to the court of King James I, wrote about coffee and its effect on human physiology at the beginning of the 17th century. Harvey, who had famously produced one of the first scientific papers that accurately described the human circulatory system, was a self-proclaimed coffee addict –

obtaining a personal supply directly through relatives engaged in the Ottoman spice trade. And Bacon, the brilliant polymath who once was suspected of being the real Shakespeare and who served as both Attorney General and Lord Chancellor, spoke with fascination about the special properties of 'Coffa' and the 'coffa-houses' of Constantinople where it was consumed without him ever having been there.

But these are only the recorded instances by writers with keen eyes for colourful detail. How many unrecorded examples of early coffee consumption in Europe were there by the multitude of seamen, travellers, merchants or soldiers who discovered the drink on their journeys, brought some back with them and either didn't or couldn't write about it?

In fact, coffee's entry into Europe came through various routes and took many guises. One of the first avenues of entry was as a pharmaceutical. In the 17th century, the connection between medicine and plants was more direct than after the chemical and biogenetics industries monopolised the treatment of illness. Doctors were trained as herbalists and dietary treatment of disease was common. The great herbariums in all the major European cities provided vital stocks of exotic plants for tinctures and infusions that were used to treat most common illnesses and the herbalist/gardeners were always on the lookout for new botanical wonders. Merchant ships often had resident naturalists aboard whose job it was to search for any new plant that would provide a better cure for some chronic malady – with which Europe back then was riddled.

Before the drink became popular in Europe, a number of Western physicians observed the medicinal uses of coffee either in their travels or through connection with colleagues in Arabia or the Levant. As early as the 1570s reports were being written on the effects of coffee by practitioners like Leonhart Rauwolff, a doctor from Augsburg, who commented that the Turks used it extensively for the treatment of stomach ailments. Others, such as Olfert Dapper, an Amsterdam physician travelling in Egypt and Persia with a group of Dutch merchants in the mid-17th century, discussed the use of coffee by Arab women as a tonic to bring on delayed menstruation. Francois Bernier, a French medic, writing from Cairo in 1654 spoke enthusiastically of coffee's remarkable power to 'strengthen the constitution and take away headaches and dizziness'.

We know, therefore, that coffee was discussed and used in Europe both as a drink and a medicine early in the 17th century by a few, clued-in and sometimes very powerful people as well as the invisible foreign population who consumed coffee in the quiet of their homes. But that tells us little about how coffee became such an important commodity a hundred years later. If coffee was used in certain port cities and academic centres in Europe for many years prior to it becoming a popular drink, what was the catalyst that finally brought it into the realm of mass consumption? Was there some 'Big Bang' or did a number of factors come into play at a particular time, lighting the fuse that sent the coffee rocket bursting into the European sky spelling out 'Drink me!' in crimson red?

In order for us to try and understand coffee's dramatic shift from an item of curiosity to a product of enormous value, we need to go beyond the written accounts of contemporaries and consider the economic and social forces at work that provided the basis for that to happen. What's crucial to understand is the extent of revolutionary change that took place in 17th century Europe. Feudalism no longer made sense as an economic model. A new world was being created but what that world was going to be wasn't yet clear.

For ordinary people who had been tied to the land and to their feudal positions, the changes taking place meant finding new modes of existence. One way of life was closing down, but another was opening up. At the same time a progressive urbanisation of Europe was taking place. People left their villages and towns, which had become moribund, for cities where life was starting to be spiced up by boundless commodities offloaded at numerous ports and distributed to urban centres along the continental rivers and coasts.

But all was not sweetness and light. Great economic shifts are never easily accomplished. The European map was being redrawn as competing forces tried to either conserve old privileges or make way for the new. In the German states the past was being torn asunder in 30 years of war. Millions died. Disease was rampant as famine and vestiges of the black plague reappeared. Millions more were on the move creating a transient population that no longer had roots in the tiny communities of their parents.

Mercantilism had become the name of the game. Trade and control of commodities was everything. The merchant class now reigned supreme and had forever taken over from the landed gentry as the real power brokers. But even they were playing in the dark as nothing had come before to guide their way. These merchant adventurers were explorers who would either make vast fortunes or sink into nothingness.

So how did coffee fit into all of this? Primarily, it was one of the fuels that ignited this amazing transformation. The financial empires being born in places like London and Amsterdam needed bright young things to energise a passage into uncharted waters. The venue of the coffeehouse was first used as a meeting place for merchants and traders who wanted a semi-public space to exchange information and to conduct business on the hoof. Like the Sufi's several centuries before, there was a drink that hit the mark – if what was required was to be awake, bright and alert. In fact the similarity between the entry of coffee into Arabia and Europe is striking. In both cases the drink was there and used almost invisibly until a certain community took it up and made it part of a ritual. We might think of the new commodity traders who formed the basis of a nascent stock exchange as the equivalent community in Northern Europe to the Sufis in Yemen. That coffee became the drink of choice for these economic gurus is not at all surprising. As with the Sufi's, it seemed to fit the bill. And as the embryonic stock exchange was searching for a venue, coffee and the coffeehouse were found to be perfectly suited for that cutting-edge business which demanded quickness of thought. All that was required was to exchange the god of the Sufis for the god of the new merchant elite – by simply adding an 'l' , turning god into gold.

Café Seller by Martin Engelbrecht, 1730. Augsburg

❖8❖

Development of the Western Coffee Culture

THE CAFÉ SYSTEM, both in Britain and much of continental Europe, had a precursor – a people's café, so to speak – before the establishment of those of bricks and mortar. They were the street cafés that existed one day and were gone the next, popping up here and there, only to move on somewhere else either to search out new business or because they were unlicensed and undesired by the authorities who tried to keep a tight handle on places of trade. But street pedlars had always been a feature of urban life. For the native poor and recently arrived immigrants, it was a way of earning a pittance with a minimal investment of cash and a maximum investment of labour.

City life in the great urban centres such as London and Paris during the 17th and 18th centuries was much like a travelling circus. The cries of street merchants selling everything under the sun punctuated the pungent air, heavy with sweat, sweets and excrement, from early morning till long after sundown. There were so many vendors hawking a vast array of goods that to make oneself known a street pedlar needed something special – either through colourful costume, mesmerising spiel or by dint of selling exotic goods that added a little twinkle to a life that might otherwise be unhappily drab.

Ferdinand Braudel in his magnificent social-economic-historical saga, *The Wheels of Commerce*, writes about the important role of pedlars – those 'merchants who carried on their backs their very meagre stock. They filled the gaps in the regular channels of distribution ... since the gaps were plentiful, so were the pedlars.' Throughout the cities and towns of Europe there was a deafening chorus. 'Anything that could be sold was carried through the streets: fritters, fruits, kindling, charcoal, raisins, celery, cooked peas, oranges...' Jacques Accarias de Serionne in his 18th century classic, *The Wealth of Holland*, wrote how the country was flooded with 'pack-carriers, pedlars and hawkers, who sell a multitude of strange goods to the rich and wealthy...'

These were, by and large, nameless people who frequented every city and town and often were the first to introduce wondrous things from far-off places to a population eager to try anything new. There were two types – the itinerant wanderer who sold whatever was at hand, then vanished with the wind, and the more stable traders who had a skill or a craft and maintained a place, a piece of turf, a pitch on some street or avenue by a well-trafficked bridge or passage. They could be fishmongers or hatters or booksellers; the streets were full of them, each wearing their own distinctive costume.

La Roque tells us about an itinerant seller who in the mid-17th century began appearing on the streets of Paris. He wrote: 'A small limping man named Candiot walked about crying "coffee". He wore a white apron and carried, fastened to his belt, a bright metal box with coffee, sugar, cups and other implements. In one hand he had a brazier with a cafetiere mounted on it, in the other a kind of water tank.'

A 1714 Prussian report on peddlers, the Packentrager, speaks of them passing through pubs and middle-class houses in the countryside, through all market towns, villages and castles, selling snuff, combs, tooth powder, beauty spots, tea and coffee. Another report from Bremen in 1720 accused peddlers of flooding the city with cheap coffee and tea.

Somewhat later in the 1730s, the German artist, Martin Engelbrecht, designed a series of lithographs of street sellers wearing the costume of their trade. One of these very intricate drawings is of a coffee vendor kitted out with his equipment – a sack of coffee strapped around his waist along with brazier and bellows, a tray with a goblet and pitcher in one hand and another tray with coffee pot and alcohol stove balanced on his head. It's a marvellous image and one wonders how the poor fellow was able to walk, let alone stand.

Did the more successful of these coffee sellers eventually set up shop somewhere with four walls and a roof? It's likely some did. We have no way of really knowing what happened in those very early years. But it seems they all had a connection with the Ottoman café culture that provided the only known model for setting up and running a coffeehouse.

Writing in the 18th century, Samuel Johnson tells us '...a Greek servant, called Pasqua, brought into England by Mr Daniel Edwards, a Turkey merchant, in 1652, to make his coffee, first set up the profession of coffeeman, and introduced the drink among us.' And an Oxford antiquarian, a contemporary of Johnson's, writes that around the same time as Pasqua, coffee was publicly sold in Oxford 'at or near the Angel at the East Gate of Oxon' by an 'outlander or Jew' named Jacob who came from somewhere in the Levant.

Many of the early London coffeehouses used some Levantine emblem as their logo and, judging by their names – like the Jerusalem, the Sultan's Head, Morat Ye Great – made a conscious effort to maintain an Ottoman appearance.

Likewise in Paris, the earliest coffeehouse was Eastern in flavour. Started by an Armenian, it drew its clientele from the 'foreign' community as well as the indigenous French who were acquainted with the Levant, like members of the Knights of Malta who frequented the place to the disdain of the Parisian middle classes.

Yet thirty years later the bourgeoisie of Paris were flocking to numerous coffee cafés, now grandiose in style and manner, and central London was close to having a coffeehouse on every street corner. Meanwhile, the coffee culture had spread to Vienna – assisted by the Ottoman invasion – as well as Hamburg and Amsterdam, where the connection with the burgeoning stock exchange was underlined by the habit of traders continuing on with their buying and selling at the coffeehouses behind the Bourse after the exchange itself had shut its doors.

This generational transition of coffee from exotic to popular is mirrored in the statistical data that comes down to us through the trade figures meticulously noted by the solemn bookkeepers and scribes of the two great trading monopolies that had established quasi-governmental status by the late 17th century – the English East India Company and the Dutch Vereenigde Oost-Indische Compagnie, otherwise known as the VOC.

In 1689, the Dutch VOC had orders for coffee from the Levant bringing in some 80,000 pounds, increasing five fold to 400,000 pounds in 1695. By 1711, the orders were up to 700,000 pounds. The English East India Company recorded orders from Mocha at around 500,000 pounds in 1711, rising to 2.5 million pounds in 1724.

During this early period all coffee that came into Europe was grown in the Yemen under the strict guidance of the Ottoman regime. But in 1684, the Dutch trade representation in Mocha was closed down due to irreconcilable difficulties with procurement and orders were re-directed to the Company's factories in Persia and Surat. The English as well began to seek new supply routes as it was becoming more and more difficult to maintain a reliable flow of good quality coffee at a consistent price for all the addicts that had been created over the period when coffee shifted from being a curiosity to a necessary part of the daily urban ritual.

What happened in those 50 odd years that created such a change? The great cities of London, Paris and Amsterdam had, of course, grown and prospered. And, as we've discussed, it was a time of dramatic economic transition. There was a subsequent need for some communal semi-public space where business could be enacted, where travellers could meet, tell stories, exchange information; where people could get out of the rain and the cold and connect.

Restaurants and diners were for meals and didn't have the easygoing ambiance of these new coffee cafés where people could come for an hour or stay all day (as many did). Outside of one's own house or a bench in a public park, where else was there? There were taverns and the gin dens, of course, but they quickly led to inebriation that ran counter to clear-headed discourse. At an energised time, when the world was being built anew, coffee would come to trump booze – at least for a certain type of new-model citizen and, even then, not without a struggle.

❖9❖

SOURCING THE BEAN

THE EXPLOSION OF the coffee culture in England, France and Holland created a demand for a consistent supply of coffee flowing to the new places of consumption. That presented a problem for the merchants who provided the stuff. As long as coffee beans were only available from Mocha or other Yemenite ports where the coffee trade was active, there was a danger that access could be turned off at the will of the caliphate.

Both the English and Dutch, who were the main European traders in coffee those days through their respective East India Companies, tended to purchase their coffee from transhipment ports on the west Indian coast in Gujarat or Malabar where they had permanent trading posts and coffee could be warehoused. However, as the coffee market was expanding so quickly it became necessary to seek out more direct sourcing to provide a certain amount of control over price and supply by buying directly from the growers – if possible.

Europeans, though, were not the most favoured nations in Yemen – partly because of the residual hostility between the Christian and Muslim religions, even if that was not as great a problem as sometimes has been suggested. More to the point was the strong arm tactics by the various European merchant fleets which used threats and intimidation, backed up by superior fire power, to demand trade advantages – a kind of gun-boat diplomacy which was unappreciated by the Yemenite sheiks who were used to a more straightforward bargaining routine based on simple bribery and corruption.

As the Red Sea trade was actually dominated by the Egyptians, Turks, Indians and Persians who were able to communicate directly as they at least attempted to speak each other's dialects, the Europeans found themselves at a distinct disadvantage when it came to negotiations. Therefore, they tended to depend on the trade intermediaries, like the Greeks, Armenians, Jews and Banyans, who were familiar with the languages and cultures of both east and west. These shadowy figures who inhabited most of the eastern trading ports became the brokers without whom few contracts could be settled. Gun boats or not, the European merchants eventually had to come to terms with the fact that they never really held the upper hand in the delicate balance of trade relations – in the Red Sea trading world, at least.

All the commercially grown coffee in those days came from the mountainous region in western Yemen. The most important market town was Beit el-Fakir in the foothills some sixty miles inland from the Red Sea. It was here that farmers, large and small, came to auction off their coffee harvests to the merchants who travelled from all over the Middle East. The vast majority of coffee sold at these auctions was bound for Egypt, Turkey, Persia and Iraq and was taken by donkey and camel from Beit el-Fakir to the Red Sea ports north of Mocha which were closer to Suez and thus cheaper to ship to the great warehouses of Cairo and Alexandria.

The European trading merchants used Mocha as their port of preference as that was the harbour they were most familiar with and where they had on and off trade representation. It worked for them as long as coffee was a minor part of their total cargo – but once coffee became a commodity of major importance the slap dash bargaining techniques of the past no longer were appropriate if they were to become key players. The problem with trading directly with Mocha was that the supply was determined by Ottoman demand as well as the occasional acts of God that led to poor harvests.

By the late 17th century it had become clear to the East Indian Company managers – especially the Dutch VOC – that other sourcing was needed if the coffee trade was to expand. At the same time, the tight control over coffee production by the Ottoman caliphate was becoming more difficult. For over a hundred years the Ottomans had kept an iron grip on the commercial use of the coffee plant but now that hold was becoming more tenuous. Curiously, it was in India that the wall of steel surrounding access to the coffee plant, making it so that no European could obtain either cuttings or fertile beans, was breeched.

But why India? This was very peculiar, especially as the Indian relationship to coffee was so ambiguous. Though coffee itself had long been an item of trade in West Indian ports, there was hardly any domestic market for it. Yet wild coffee plants had been observed growing in the foothills near the Malabar Coast by both the English and the Dutch who had set up trading posts in Cochin. How did they get there?

According to legend, the coffee plant was brought to India in 1670 by Saint Baba Budan after a visit to Yemen where he discovered coffee and 'acquired' seven beans which he germinated and then introduced into the highlands near Chikmagalur. Legends aside, we can probably surmise that coffee groves were started by sailors, merchants or travelling mystics plying the Red Sea trade routes – most likely Muslims, perhaps Sufis, who had journeyed to Yemen and brought back with them viable seeds which they planted so as to maintain their own source for brewing up the drink they had come to love.

So even though the coffee plant was closely guarded in Yemen, in India it was there for the taking. And once noted by Dutch intelligence that here was a supply uncontrolled by Ottoman sentinels, the idea finally percolated through to the company shareholders in Amsterdam that there might be a way around the conundrum of dependency on

Yemen as their one and only source for the precious coffee bean.

Growing coffee isn't easy. Not only does it take very specialised knowledge – and there was yet no European with experience growing the stuff – but it also takes a unique environment for coffee to prosper. Farming coffee commercially in Southern India was a possibility, of course, and later that would indeed happen. But in the 17th century, the coffee grown there was sparse and uncommercial. Besides, the Dutch didn't control Malabar – certainly not to the extent that they could have organised coffee plantations. But they did control an island in the Indian Ocean far to the east in a tropical region with cool volcanic mountains, where coffee might grow very well. That island was Java, part of the Indonesian archipelago, where the Portuguese once held sway until the Dutch took over their poorly fortified trading stations.

View of Mocha. Engraving by Adriaen Matham, 1616

❖10❖

COFFEE IS COLONISED

ESTABLISHING COFFEE FARMS in Java was a shift from everything that had happened in the past. Up until that point of departure, when the plant was uprooted from its native soil, there had always been a connection between consumer and producer. Coffee in the Yemen was grown commercially, but the product was deeply embedded in the country and when the coffee trade expanded, it continued to be based in a culture that had nurtured it. In other words, coffee production in Yemen was indigenous to a community, wasn't separate from it, and even though there was an economic basis to coffee production, there was an overriding understanding that coffee was integral to a way of life and that the grower was consciously part of a chain that led to a ritualised consumption. Despite the fact that coffee had long since left the Sufi dakhir, the relationship of coffee to the Middle-Eastern communities made it more than simply a drink. Coffee in the Ottoman world was a way of life and the growing of coffee in Yemen was integral to the system.

The production of coffee in Java was different. Here, there was no coffee culture to speak of. The people who grew it were indentured servants who had no relationship to the plant they were forced to tend and were obliged to harvest a pre-determined yield.

The frequenters of a coffeehouse in Istanbul may not have known precisely where their coffee came from, but they intuitively understood that it was part of a chain that connected them to some unifying idea, even if there were differences of opinion as to what that unifying idea actually was. But the coffee growers in Yemen were part of that unifying idea as well. There might have been bribery and corruption and a kind of exploitation within the Ottoman coffee trade, but the trade, itself, was always linked to an overriding notion that gave a higher purpose to even the rougher aspects of the coffee business. This concept was not about religious dogma but had to do with a cultural unification that had been developed over hundreds of years.

Coffee production in Java was based on brutal economics pure and simple. There was a commercial need to produce coffee that was good enough to compete with the Yemeni exports. But that was a question of agronomics. We might assume there was no way an indentured Javanese farmer who was growing coffee under the threat of a cosh was going to produce coffee beans anywhere near the quality that was grown in the Yemeni mountains by small planters whose ancestors had passed down to them both knowledge and commitment.

And yet there were other factors at work that made this colonised agricultural system an effective supplier to those Europeans craving the bean. First and foremost was the fact that coffee was a rapidly expanding commodity and that most of the new consumers who never tasted coffee before had no basis for comparison. Secondly, the early coffee shops were not catering to sophisticated tastes and made coffee from beans that were often old and mildewed anyway. Thirdly, coffee was a bitter brew – especially the way early coffeehouses cooked it. However, the entry of cheap sugar onto the market made it so that even the worst coffee could become palatable and still give consumers the required buzz. Fourthly, and perhaps most important, all the wonderful new products that were entering the European market came from somewhere else – and few people knew where that somewhere was.

Yet, strangely enough, as ironic as it may seem given everything above, over the years coffee from Yemen got worse and coffee from Java got better. And this strange turn of events had nothing to do with the brutality of production. It just so happened that the coffee plant liked the volcanic soil in the Javanese foothills, which turned out to be an exceptionally good environment. And, at the same time, the periodic droughts in Yemen had created conditions that were not so beneficial for the plant. Which is only to say that plants are plants and humans are humans. We might not like what certain societies have on offer, but the world of plants has its own concerns. The Dutch colonialists went a long way toward destroying the native ecology in Java causing environmental havoc that scars what once was once seen as an island paradise (though I use that word advisedly since paradise and trouble often go hand in hand). But, in good years and with proper care, Javanese coffee still ranks with the best.

The Javanese coffee experiment wasn't an easy birth. It took bull-headed determination on the part of the company overlords to see it through. The investment in time, money and people was enormous. It was years before the plant could be propagated and then a further four years before the first beans could be harvested. Also, a workable system of farming had to be managed without the guidance of anyone who had experience running a coffee plantation.

And who was to grow it anyway? Unlike the plantations set up in the Caribbean, there wasn't a pool of slaves to choose from. The Dutch were forced to use a form of contract labour, bringing in thousands of Chinese and natives from other islands in the Indonesian archipelago. Fortunately for the Dutch colonialists – if not for the people colonised – there had been other crops that were grown and traded that provided a template for the newly created coffee farms. These were the crops grown for the lucrative spice trade. Chief among them was nutmeg, grown extensively and quite successfully on the Banda islands, many of whose inhabitants were forcefully transported over 1000 miles to Java – though few survived.

It must be said that the Dutch were neither more nor less brutal than any of the other European nations that became part of the colonial system. Yet the Dutch Republic was, if anything, a model of tolerance and democracy – for the 17th and 18th centuries, at least. It was a nation itself built by immigrants and refugees. The citizens at home, who benefited from the massive wealth coming back to Holland by dint of the East Indian trade, were hardly aware of the ramifications. It wasn't until 1860 and the publication of *Max Havelaar: Or the Coffee Auctions of the Dutch Trading Company* by Multatuli that most Dutch people became conscious of the dreadful consequences of colonialism and how much their cup of coffee truly cost in terms of human abuse.

The successful propagation of the coffee plant outside its native habitat caused a great deal of excitement, not only in the other European trading conglomerates but also within the scientific communities. It wasn't long before arrangements were made to send cuttings to Amsterdam's great botanical gardens, the Hortus Bontanicus, where sometime in the first decade of the 18th century, coffee was triumphantly grown on European soil.

In the history of coffee, this was a moment to savour. Coffee had been liberated (or stolen) from its natural homeland and was successfully grown to maturity in northern Europe. Of course it was nurtured to fruition by the cleverest, most experienced and exceptionally talented gardeners but, even so, this was a monumental achievement.

When word leaked out that this amazing feat had actually been accomplished, it didn't take long before requests came from gardens throughout Europe for cuttings of their own. As far as we know, only one request was fulfilled. That request was the most curious of all. And the fact that it was fulfilled in 1714 is one of those extraordinary historical puzzles yet to be solved. Because the request was from the King of France, Louis XIV, a keen gardener and amateur scientist, yes, but also the head of a nation that, next to England, was the primary trading competitor of the Dutch. And this plant cutting the Statholder of Amsterdam so graciously forwarded to King Louis, would, in a few short years, see its progeny populate the Caribbean, central and south America – to the detriment of the very people who gifted it.

Earlier in the book we spoke of the great coffee historian, la Roque, at the Jardin des Plants in Paris as he stood admiring the coffee tree that had been grown from the cutting sent to Louis XIV and the excitement this scene engendered. But the full impact of that event couldn't possibly have made itself known to him, because who could have imagined what happened next?

❖11❖

THE GENIE UNCORKED AND
UNBOTTLED

THE GAME WAS afoot. Whatever agreement the French and Dutch botanists had between themselves in the rarefied world of hothouses and exotic vegetation was null and void when it came to the nuts and bolts of global economics. Once the French had mastered the technique of growing the coffee plant to maturity, there was no holding back. Promises were one thing; business was another. And, as the 18th century lurched forward, the world was appearing more and more – from the perspective of the great European powers – like one gigantic garden, the produce of which was there for the taking by whoever got there first and planted it.

The Eastern trade routes might have been dominated by the Dutch in the early 1700s, with the French confined mainly to their small outpost in Pondicherry, but to the west were the glittering islands of the Caribbean, divided like little jewels between the competing colonial powers. Having been brutally cleansed of indigenous peoples some years before, those islands controlled by France, were repopulated, in a large part, by Huguenots forced into exile by the revocation of the Treaty of Nantes which had up until 1685 given political and civil rights to Protestants. Many came as indentured servants to work in the sugar and tobacco plantations – just as the Dutch colonies attracted immigrant Jews who had come as refugees to Holland by way of Portugal and the English islands drew in populations of debtors who chose exile instead of prison.

The others who came to work these new plantations hadn't even the modicum of choice given to the Huguenots and other white Europeans who might have been escaping something worse in Europe. They were the brutalised human cargos who, along with the colonial produce of tobacco, sugar, cotton and, soon, coffee, were making the mercantile powers of France, Britain and Holland extraordinarily rich. Whereas in the East, the commodity trade was based on the exploitation of the native populations, in the West it was powered by slaves shipped from Africa by way of cities like Nantes in France and Liverpool in England.

The taste of coffee had been firmly implanted in urban Europe. And now that sugar had developed into a commodity of mass consumption, the coffee drink was becoming more palatable to a larger population. By the second decade of the 1700s, the coffeehouse was a fixture in all the major cities. Imports of coffee were expanding by leaps and bounds. So it was clear to those whose ear was tuned to the commodity trade that the time was ripe for this Arabian drink to be fully exploited. The tropical islands of the Caribbean lay beckoning and

France now had the plant in its possession. The only thing standing in the way of starting up West Indian coffee farms was the problem of getting it there.

Shipping a coffee plant over 4,000 miles from France to its outposts in the Caribbean was not as easy in the early 1700s as it is today. In fact, up until 1829 and the invention of the Wardian Case – a glass enclosed terrarium especially designed for transporting plants across oceans – the vast majority didn't survive long sea voyages. The Atlantic was an especially perilous crossing for uprooted flora that required protection from winds and saltwater sprays but needed exposure to light and the warmth of the sun.

Thus the journey of Gabriel de Clieu, the French naval officer who brought one of the coffee trees from the Jardin des Plants in Paris to Martinique in 1720 is celebrated as a glorious achievement by both merchants and botanists as well as all those who celebrate anything French. For this plant which de Clieu nurtured on a perilous voyage with loving care, feeding it (according to his later writings) water from his own meagre rations, protecting it from storms and Dutch commercial agents, became sanctified (if a coffee plant could become a saint, this one was high on the list) as the mother of all the subsequent coffee trees in the Western Hemisphere. A bit hyperbolic to be sure, considering that the Dutch and English were able to set up coffee plantations in their respective Caribbean colonies at about the same time – and who really knows how many coffee plants were floating around by then. But it does have the appeal of being a good story and one which will be, I'm sure, retold for eternity (or for as long as people write coffee books).

What's perhaps even more remarkable than getting the coffee tree across the ocean to its new island home in the Caribbean sun, is how well it did there. Cuttings from that one tree, planted by de Clieu himself (or so he claimed) produced hundreds more. Soon trees were planted all over the island and by 1777 Martinique was said to be home to over 18 million. Coffee farming quickly spilled over to the neighbouring island of Guadeloupe.

Meanwhile, the Dutch were busily planting coffee trees of their own in Surinam, their main West Indian colony sitting uneasily between the two Guyanas – a god-forsaken lump of land, according to some of the early settlers or a place of astounding beauty, according to others. Whatever way they pictured it, living there was a harsh existence. The vast majority of the population were slaves brought in holds of the same ships that would take the Caribbean coffee and sugar, produced by their labour, to Europe and then, loading up with manufactured goods, would journey back to Africa to trade for more slaves – who, once in Surinam, generally survived no more than six years. They were simply seen as farming equipment that wore out and was periodically replaced, amortised in profit and loss statements by bored accountants in Holland, France and England.

Most of the white colonists didn't fare that well either, often dying of insatiable tropical diseases to which they had less resistance than their African field workers. But coffee was a possible route to wealth with a smaller investment needed to start a coffee farm than to set up a sugar processing mill. In 1761 there were 280 coffee plantations in Surinam. From the mid-1700s, large harvests were regularly sent back to the ports of Amsterdam and Rotterdam – reaching about 12 million pounds per annum by 1770.

From Surinam, coffee spread to the neighbouring French colony of Cayenne – later known as French Guyana – supposedly brought there by marauding French soldiers or deserting Dutch ones, depending on who was telling the story. Cayenne never became a big player in the sugar boom. Under populated and remote, it fascinated the French more as the fabled gateway to El Dorado than as a permanent settlement itself. Actually, it worked rather in reverse with Cayenne acting as an entry point for other interests that would eventually change the locus of the coffee industry due south and transform the Caribbean coffee nations into minnows compared to the colossus that was to rise up from the jungle just beyond. But that was yet some years off. In the early part of the 18th century it was these new coffee plantations, dotted around the Caribbean sea, which shortly would include Jamaica, Haiti, Dominica, Cuba and Puerto Rico as well as any landfall that had volcanic highlands and could support a settlement of European colonists, no matter how small, along with the requisite number of manacled Africans.

Interestingly, there was another bean of note that resided in the forests of Martinique when coffee arrived. Indigenous to South America, it had been brought to the Caribbean islands as an early plantation crop, along with sugar cane which provided the additive that made chocolate more palatable to European tastes. Cacao had been used in Europe since the early 16th century as a drink by lords and ladies intrigued by the fanciful stories of Montezuma whose cities had been plundered by marauding conquistadors while he and his court drank frothy glass after glass of the stuff. Prohibitively expensive for all but the social elite until the late 17th century, chocolate was starting to make inroads amongst the middle classes about the same time as the emergence of coffee – the first dedicated chocolate house being set up in London in 1657.

In one of those curious moments of serendipity, coffee was brought to Martinique just as the cacao crops were starting to fail due to a combination of foraging insects, disease and a period of violent weather that had laid waste to many of the cacao plantations. The coffee tree was found to be an easy replacement and far more suitable to the soil and climate. But, in the end, it was simply a matter of economics. From the point of view of those who financed these growing agricultural ventures – the big money investors who had no interest in or understanding of plants or where they came from except as products of trade – it didn't matter if Martinique provided beans for chocolate or coffee or whatever else might be both marketable and addictive. From the point of view of the grower, however, a wrong choice of plantation crop could spell disaster – not only for them as individuals but for everyone inhabiting those crypto-nations. Later, for example, certain parts of Central America would bet on indigo which made vast fortunes for the planters but then forced them into bankruptcy when the market collapsed after the emerging chemical industry started pumping out artificial dyes. Again, coffee came to the rescue – for a while, that is, until the price of coffee collapsed. But that story comes later and has to do with Phase Two of coffee's progressive globalisation and the rise and fall of the coffee nations.

There is one other place that features in this discussion of the early coffee trade that was quickly moving away from its Ottoman origins. Along with the Eastern outpost of Java and the Western plantations based in and around the Caribbean, a new area of coffee production had suddenly become important.

That was the French island of Reunion – known then as Ile Bourbon.

It was a most unlikely place. Set in the middle of nowhere, 200 kilometres southwest of Mauritius, its nearest neighbour, Ile Bourbon was one of those rare pieces of Indian Ocean real estate that actually had been uninhabited. Up until the 18th century, it was known only as a place for shipwrecked sailors or abandoned mutineers. Then a passing French merchant ship that was involved in the Yemeni trade, discovered the island and concluded that the tropical climate, mountainous terrain and rich, volcanic soil, seemed to be perfectly suited for the cultivation of coffee.

In 1715 some coffee trees were brought there from Yemen and the first plantations started by Europeans in the East – outside of Java – was born. How the coffee trees were purchased, we don't know as up till then the Yemeni lock on coffee plants had been exceptionally tight. Perhaps, by then, as coffee had been growing outside of Yemen for a while, even the Ottoman overseers realised the game was up and that it was better to take what they could get in cold, hard cash rather than keep an obsessive watch over their coffee plants after the bean had already bolted. Or maybe – just as likely – the French were able to grease some itchy palms at a time when the empire was fading slowly into the setting sun.

But the curiosity of Bourbon doesn't end there. It was later discovered that the island harboured wild coffee trees. How they got there, no one knew. The island was too remote for there to have been any botanical flying carpet that dropped a bunch of pregnant seeds. It can only be assumed that Ile Bourbon was once a stopping off point for Arab traders who planted coffee trees to satisfy their need for the beautiful bean during the times they were waiting, becalmed.

Bourbon coffee came to be a favourite of the French aristocracy as well as the growing army of caffeine addicted artists and writers, such as Balzac who, according to his biographer, carried a leather pouch around with him everywhere he went which contained a supply of Café Bourbon along with a portable grinder.

18th century Parisian café. Musée Carnavalet, Paris

12

COFFEEHOUSES IN THE 18TH CENTURY

ONE OF THE difficulties in examining the development of the coffeehouse or café is not seeing it in context of other things. In that respect, it's of interest to look at 'café' as an idea rather than simply an enclosure where a certain drink was served.

Coffee cultures evolved in many different ways throughout Europe. In countries without major seaports, like Austria, the café as we have come to know it developed differently than in France. Italy, which became the model for café culture in America during the later part of the 20th century, didn't really generate much interest in the coffeehouse until the 1800s. Yet Venice, because of its economic relationship with the spice trade and its proximity to the Ottoman world, had one of the earliest European coffee cultures – though it didn't develop the kind of vibrant café life in the 18th century as was taking place in England and France.

I suspect that the actual consumption of coffee in Italy (or the lands that were to become Italy) over the 1700s was as great as anywhere in Europe. It's just that the coffee cultures there weren't considered exciting and new as they were in England and France since the Ottoman world wasn't as foreign to them as it was to the Northern Europeans. Men with turbans and beards were not an unfamiliar sight around Piazza San Marco in Venice nor in Genoa, Naples, Livorno or Syracuse. The cosmopolitan feel that one would have experienced in those cities was related to an age-old relationship with Turkey and the Levant. The same is true with Marseille in France, which probably had a coffee culture that existed from the late 16th century without much note being made of it.

But all major cities in Europe had parallel worlds as they integrated the products that accompanied the explosion of trade. Along with the new commodities came cultures and ideas that enwrapped them like an invisible skin. Coffee, nutmeg, silks and pepper all had stories to tell about where they came from, the people who nurtured them and how they were used in distant lands. It's simply that the Mediterranean world had heard these stories and had tasted the fruits of the East long before Northern Europe did. So what was exotic in London, was hardly so in Venice. People didn't write with excitement about things that had become commonplace to them.

The German speaking countries were another case where coffee was known but cafés were slow in coming. Coffee was used there quite early on, not only in the port cities such as Hamburg, but even inland where the coffee drink had been forcibly brought by marauding soldiers marching along the Spanish Road which led from Italy to the Netherlands. The Ottomans, themselves, brought tons of coffee to the very gates of Vienna, their precious rations left by Turkish troops when they retreated south. Soldiers in those days were paid through pillage and plunder, but what was plundered one place was often left somewhere else. The story of how something gets someplace is rarely straightforward.

In the 17th century, coffee entered Germany almost exclusively through the Ottoman supply chain by way of Italy and southern France – most typically, Marseille. But by the mid-18th century imports were mainly from the Caribbean with coffee arriving via Bordeaux, London or Amsterdam to Hamburg, and then distributed inland through coffee brokers in Bremen and Leipzig.

German commodity historians have indicated that it was only around the mid-18th century with new supplies of coffee coming from the West Indies that prices declined, thus making it possible for a wider section of the population to start consuming coffee on a regular basis. However it was mainly in the northern cities that coffee became widely used. In the south, it was far less popular except in university towns.

The grand cafés of the 19th century that flourished in Berlin, Vienna, Budapest, Prague and all throughout central Europe mirrored the transition that took place in urban life that was generated by political, social and economic changes brought on by a multicultural transformation. The features of the scintillating café world that emerged there will be discussed later, but for now it's enough to say that the coffee culture that became so predominant in Austro-Hungary and Germany didn't come out of thin air. Coffee was used extensively in that area of Europe before a vibrant, middle-class café culture became predominant. Proto-cafés were already emerging on the streets, in people's homes and in semi-public spaces that served coffee without being classified as an actual coffeehouse. For instance, *kaffeekranzchen* – or coffee circles – became an important part of German social life in the late 17th and early 18th centuries. It was said that these coffee klatches helped transform the image of women in German society and was even one of the principal reasons that the internal architecture of the middle-class house was redefined, with parlours – where coffee would be served – now becoming an essential room in the bourgeois household.

Even so the number of coffeehouses in German cities grew very gradually. Hamburg, for example, started with six in 1700 and increased that number only to twenty in 1800. In Frankfurt they grew even more slowly; as late as 1848 there were only seven coffeehouses registered as official (which begs the question of how many unofficial ones existed).

But it was different in England. A continental visitor to London in the early 1700s wrote with fascination about the prodigious number of coffeehouses he observed. After commenting that 'the outsides have nothing remarkable or worth describing,' he went on to say: 'These coffeehouses are the constant rendezvous for men of business as well as the idle people so that a man is sooner asked about his coffeehouse than his lodgings ... in other respects they are loathsome, full of smoke, like a guard room and as much crowded. I believe 'tis these places that furnish the inhabitants with slander for there one hears exact accounts of everything done in town as if it were but a village.'

An illustration of a typical London coffeehouse of the 1700s shows its domestic economy but also its hominess – the roaring fire with cauldrons of water on the boil, rows of long tables and wooden stools and the grandly dressed dame de comptoir – more French than English in appearance – who stood behind the payment kiosk where customers would leave their entry coin – a copper penny – and order their coffee for two pennies more.

Compared to what was happening in Paris, this scene looked a bit grotty and probably accounts for the rather snide comments made by the continental observer quoted above. Writing about Paris of the same period, la Roque tells how the French had learned 'to furnish the coffee shops with tapestries, large mirrors, pictures, marble tables and chandeliers ... which was first done in the market of St Germain ... these shops have become finely furnished drawing rooms; much imitated by everyone and in mutual competition, they have become meeting places for many of the more distinguished people who wish to refresh themselves with a cup of coffee in pleasant conversation. Writers and serious people have taken a liking to these meeting places which are so suitable for learned dialogues without constraint and social ceremony so to speak for pure pleasure ... One can say that these coffee rooms have become the greatest ornament of the markets.'

In fact, it was both in England and France that a vibrant café/coffeehouse culture emerged in the 18th century – for different reasons, with different social and architectural structures and headed in different directions: England from a culture of openness to exclusivity, from the people's café to the private club; France from mirrored palaces for the bourgeoisie to smoky dens of revolution.

According to Walter Besant, in his monumental series on the social history of London, 'a coffeehouse, was classified according to its frequenters. In the City rich merchants alone ventured to enter certain of the coffeehouses where they transacted business more privately and more expeditiously than on the Exchange ... In all alike the visitor put down his penny and went in, taking his own seat if he was an habitué; he called for a cup of tea or coffee and paid his two pence for it ... he was expected to talk with his neighbour whether he knew him or not. Men went to certain coffeehouses in order to meet the well-known poets and writers ... as Pope went in search of Dryden. The daily papers and the pamphlets of the day were taken in. Some of the coffeehouses, but not the more respectable, allowed the use of tobacco...'

The 18th century English coffeehouse, as Besant emphasised, was still strongly connected to its origins as a free-wheeling, intelligence-driven, commercial marketplace. 'At the coffee-houses were held auctions as at Sheffield's, where in 1700 were the book auctions. Men met for the transaction of business in these places; thus I have some of the accounts of the meetings of booksellers when they joined to share risks, or sold, or exchanged, or bought "copies," meaning copyrights ; bankrupts met their creditors in the coffee-houses...'

Certainly, a noteworthy aspect of the 18th century coffeehouse was its relationship to the growing book and newspaper trade. Authors, journalists and publishers made various coffeehouses their home. But the kind of atmosphere that prevailed in these writerly coffee retreats was very different from the literary cafés that became prevalent later on the continent. The English made theirs into a sort of cut-and-thrust debating society where one man would try to become king of the mountain. Besant writes, 'The coffee-houses were great schools of conversation. A man had to hold his own against a whole roomful of men eager to show their wit. The custom encouraged readiness and clearness of expression and of thought. Younger men did not venture to speak in some coffee-houses. And it is not sufficiently understood, in reading Johnson's sententious phrases, that his words were often spoken in a coffee-house so as to be heard by the whole listening room. So Dryden delivered his judgments, and was admired and worshipped by the younger men, as the oracle of the coffee-house. They, indeed, sat mute, diffident, afraid to speak in so great a presence; or, if they hazarded an opinion, did so with the greatest diffidence, and congratulated themselves afterwards if it had been favourably received.'

Writing in 1882, the social historian, John Ashton, underlined the importance of the English coffeehouse at the beginning of the 1700s, proclaiming that it was 'the centre of news, the rendezvous for appointments, the mart for business men ... the haunt of the wit and the man of fashion'.

Ashton talks of levelling the social classes, referring to the coffeehouse as 'a neutral meeting-ground for all men' but qualifying these communal inclinations by noting that the patrons 'naturally assorted themselves, like to like', suggesting, rather in jest, that a man of high position might rub shoulders with a highwayman – though the highwaymen probably couldn't have held a candle to some of the fancy financiers who spent their days drifting between coffeehouses selling creative investment ventures that usually ended up like the South Sea

Bubble, emptying the pockets of the get-rich-quick dreamers without having to bother with a pistol.

But being a good Victorian, Ashton was at pains to point out that 'the excellent rules in force, and the good common sense of the frequenters, prevented any ill effects from this admixture of classes.' Still, he claims, 'all were equal, and took the first seat which came to hand. If a man swore, he was fined one shilling, and if he began a quarrel he was fined "dishes" round. Discussion on religion was prohibited, no card-playing or dicing allowed, and no wager might be made exceeding 5 shillings. These were the simple rules generally used, and, if they were only complied with, all must have felt the benefit of such a mild despotism.'

Of course, this was a 19th century middle-class take on the populist tendencies of the 18th century English coffeehouse. By Ashton's time the coffeehouse of Queen Anne's day had long since faded and the class-ridden private club had taken over from the old drop-a-penny-in-the-dish, open to all, coffeehouse culture.

Just several decades after Ashton, Jack London would write in his exploration of the East End about the down-at-the-mouth coffeehouses he observed: 'Working-men, in the main, frequent these places, and greasy, dirty places they are, without one thing about them to cherish decency in a man or put self-respect into him... You cannot obtain coffee in such a place for love or money. True, you may call for coffee, and they will have brought you something in a cup purporting to be coffee, and you will taste it and be disillusioned, for coffee it certainly is not.' This, while the toffs in Pall Mall ate truffles on toast washed down with best Arabica.

The heyday of the English coffeehouse was, in fact, a brief phenomenon and in a perpetual state of decline as the 1700s came to a close, not to be revitalised until the 20th century (except for the curious 19th century temperance cafe that will be discussed later). However, even as the private clubs were condemning the populist notion of the coffeehouse to its fate, another aspect of the new society began to emerge. Besant summed it up rather nicely (if we can forgive his class-ridden nonsense): 'As the coffee-house rapidly ceased to be a place of resort for people of the better kind, it acquired a new lease of life when the demand for newspapers and the habit of reading newspapers descended the social ladder and therefore increased enormously. They were then frequented by men who came, not to talk, but to read; the smaller tradesmen and the better class of mechanic now came to the coffee-house, called for a cup of coffee, and with it the daily paper, which they could not afford to take in. Every coffee-house took three or four papers; there seems to have been in this latter phase of the once social institution no general conversation. The coffee-house as a place of resort and conversation gradually declined; one can hardly say why, except that all human institutions do decay. Perhaps manners declined; the leaders in literature ceased to be seen there, the city clerk began to crowd in; the tavern and the club drew men from the coffee-house.'

In Paris the early café concept based on large, open rooms with ornate furnishings – crystal chandeliers, fine tapestries, mirrored ceilings, velvet curtains – first established by the Procope in St Germain, became the template for hundreds more, usually set up adjacent to the bustling markets. Here, little marble tables surrounded by dainty chairs rather than long splintery communal benches of the English coffeehouse defined the space and how it was used. The free-wheeling merchant adventurers looking for business connections, their ears perked for information leading to quick and easy deals, might have felt just as uncomfortable in the sumptuously flamboyant Parisian cafés as the French bourgeoisie would at London's penny palaces.

The grand cafés of Paris which appealed to the likes of Voltaire and Diderot in the early part of the 18th century soon evolved as had the cafés on the other side of the channel. The social explosion that was leading inevitably to the great revolution of 1789, had its mirror in the extension of the café culture. Parisian cafés became heavily politicised. Royalists and Republicans, alike, established their territory within cafés of note, turning them into centres of vigorous debate and shadowy intrigue.

Francis Blagdon, an Englishman living in Paris, sent several letters back home that talked of the Paris coffeehouse a few years after the revolution. 'Their number has been reckoned to exceed seven hundred,' he wrote, 'but they are very far from enjoying a comparative degree of reputation... Except a few resorted to by the literati or wits of the day, or by military officers, they are, in general, the rendezvous of the idle, and the refuge of the needy.'

The proletarianisation of the Parisian coffeehouse came in conjunction with the dramatic restructuring of urban space as a consequence of the 1789 revolution. Poverty was not annihilated; it simply found a home off the pavement. As Blagdon wrote, 'a frequenter of a coffeehouse scarcely ever lights a fire in his own lodging during the whole winter. No sooner has he quitted his bed, and equipped himself for the day, than he repairs to his accustomed haunt, where he arrives about ten o'clock in the morning, and remains till eleven at night, the hour at which coffeehouses are shut ...'

Before leaving our discussion of the 18th century, it should be noted that even though the coffeehouse began as an institution that in many ways helped develop the cosmopolitan nature of the urban landscape by establishing a space which was uniquely inclusive and did much to break down social, ethnic and political divides, there was one group of people who were still largely excluded – and that was women.

Unlike the Moslem world, Northern Europe had few codified prohibitions that meant women were banned by law. Instead, the cultural mores of the time meant that women were excluded more on the basis of custom and practice. And even that had its exceptions.

Just as the Ottoman cafés were known to hire attractive boys to lure clients into a particular coffeehouse, English and French cafés quite openly used sex appeal to bring in customers. In the 18th century there was no objection to having a good looking woman behind the coffee counter – in fact, cafés were more often noted for the charms of the women they employed than for the quality of their fare, often using women like sweeteners to entice sugar-deprived men.

But as the intellectual ferment of the period was acted out in the cafés, the political and social revolutions that saw women play a leading role meant they could hardly be excluded as customers from the very place the seeds of change were being sown.

In fact, even earlier in the 18th century women were sometimes present amongst the literary and artistic circles that met at various cafés; they simply dressed themselves like men, as was the case with Voltaire's lover – Emilie du Chatelet, who became a regular at Café Gradot.

13

A TALE OF TWO COUNTRIES: HAITI AND CEYLON

AS NEW PRODUCTION outlets came on line and as the coffee culture dispersed throughout Europe with cafés becoming a typical part of most urban scenes, the market for coffee beans grew exponentially to the point that the emerging sources in the Caribbean could hardly keep pace with demand that was far exceeding supply. Great opportunities for expansion existed.

Coffee by now had reached the popular classes but was still far too expensive for most people to drink on a regular basis. Then something happened that changed the game and shifted the centre of production once more – but this time unleashing a behemoth that would transform the way coffee was grown, processed and sold for generations to come.

This chapter is the story of two countries that each played a crucial role in the development of the coffee saga in the late 18th and early 19th centuries: Haiti and Ceylon. Both of these places had, at a certain time, been an important coffee producer and each developed the coffee culture in a different way. But by the end of the 19th century only one country stood out in the coffee trade, eventually becoming a giant in the coffee-producing world. However, in the final decades of the 18th century, right up to the French revolution, if you were going to bet on the most likely place to be the world's foremost coffee empire, you would have probably put your money on Haiti. And in the middle part of the 19th century, you might very well have bet on Ceylon.

Haiti wasn't the first island in the Caribbean to grow coffee. In fact, when plantations were initially started there it wasn't yet 'Haiti' but Saint-Dominigue, the western third of the island of Hispaniola which had been divided between France and Spain in one of those appalling treaties that carved up the 'new world' like a ripe piece of fruit for shared colonial consumption.

Hispaniola was, of course, the place Columbus 'discovered' on one of his early voyages scouting out new territories to loot for the Spanish Empire. In those days it was gold and other precious minerals that was desired by the Crown. But Columbus wrote such glowing reports of this Caribbean jewel with its amazingly fertile soil and the most perfect harbours he had ever seen, that a colony was soon set up. Unfortunately, this island jewel was already occupied by people who had been there for many centuries. Within a few years the native population were annihilated along with their habitat and a more 'compliant' work force was brought in from Africa to tend the new plantations that soon would be set up.

In the Caribbean, as elsewhere in the Americas, clearing of the land by the colonial powers meant that aboriginal peoples were viewed something like weeds to be uprooted so that new gardens of earthly delights could prosper (for the benefit of Europeans). It might seem absurdly uneconomic to wipe out a potential labour force that was already there, only to ship in another from thousands of miles away. But from a callously mercantilist point of view, it wasn't. The theory and practice of colonial slavery assumed that it was always more problematic enslaving people in their own territory than to bring in others who were torn from their families and their ancestral homes, taking them so far away they could never hope to return, and keeping them desperate, isolated and bewildered. It required that indigenous cultures be replaced by human 'drones' whose past had been obliterated, overseen by the culture of the whip where hard labour became a less painful option than idleness. Like wild horses, new slaves were seen as simply needing to be broken. This couldn't be done to the native inhabitants who knew every inch of their land and who would never completely acquiesce to the demands of those they saw as invaders. Therefore it was more expedient and simply more cost-effective to kill them off and ship in others having no connection to the strange place they were brought. Unlike the native population, this tyrannized human cargo didn't see the European colonists as occupiers but masters who, as far as they knew, had always been there. That, in essence, was the brutal rationale of the slave trade that became the muscle to farm the plantations providing Europe with coffee, sugar, cotton and tobacco. And, for a while, it worked – except in the land that would come to be known as Haiti.

By the 18th century, Saint-Domingue was the richest colony in the Caribbean, producing 60 percent of all the coffee consumed in Europe and exporting more sugar and coffee than all of the British West Indies combined. Nearly 40,000 Europeans, mainly French, had set up farms producing coffee, sugar, cotton and indigo – plantations that were worked by three quarters of a million African slaves. A writer visiting Saint-Domingue in the 1780s commented that the planters were living on the edge of a volcano – both physically and metaphorically. He was both right and prescient. A little over a decade later, the colonists had either fled to neighbouring countries or had been slaughtered in a bloody slave revolt. Plantations were burned to the ground. The black republic of Haiti was about to be born, but the coffee empire of Saint-Domingue had come to an end.

Why was it on Haiti rather than the rest of the Caribbean islands that the slaves rebelled and the plantation economy came to a grinding halt? Partly it had to do with the unique demographic make-up of Saint-Domingue, but mainly it was a response to what was happening back in Europe as the popular struggles of the 18th century were about to reach their climax.

Over the years, Saint-Domingue had developed a significant mixed-race population. Children of liaisons between French planters and slaves were (if male) often adopted by the slave owner and sent to France for their education. Educated, free and often propertied, they were strongly influenced by the revolutionary fervour gripping France as the century was coming to an end. Certainly many of them would have participated in the great debates taking place in Parisian coffeehouses regarding the rights of man and the irony could hardly have escaped them that the very coffee fuelling their discourse had been produced back home thanks to the manacled prowess of their enslaved relatives who had no rights whatsoever.

These educated mulattos came to form a distinct class within the society of Saint-Domingue. And when the French Revolution finally came in 1789, some were anxious to convey the radical spirit of universal liberty. Even before the revolution actually transpired, the slaves of French planters were filled with expectation and hope as rumours had spread that King Louis XVI had mandated all slaves in his dominion would have three days off a week from servitude. The rumour proved false, but the fires of freedom once lit were difficult to curtail.

The rebellion that followed came out of a time of intense social and economic readjustment and a century of extreme abuse suffered by enslaved Africans in a country where they were vastly in the majority and where there was a significant number of mixed-race freemen who served as a black intelligentsia and could transmit the radical ideas expounded during the French Revolution.

Back in France, the fine ideals articulated in the statements concerning the rights of man, were quickly quashed and qualified both by race and gender. What followed in Saint-Domingue was an explosion of intense anger resulting in horrific acts of revenge from which the Haitian coffee trade could never recover.

The destruction of the coffee trade in Haiti left the door open for a new entry into the bean production business. The island nations that were growing coffee at the time were ill equipped to increase production, both through limitation of adequate land – as the coffee plant needed certain specific conditions regarding soil and altitude – and people to grow it. But, at the same time, the price of coffee was rising quickly due to shortage and so the market was exceptionally buoyant. The only question was, where would the next coffee empire be located?

The sun was rising in the East once more. England had long been involved in the Indian coffee trade but even though some plantations had been started in the Mysore, it was not yet a major area of production

117

in the early years of the 19th century. However, to the south, just a stone's throw from Kerala, was an island kingdom that seemed well suited for the kind of tropical plants that needed those special conditions of long-lasting light, fine volcanic soil, cool mountain air and the moistness of a morning mist that freshens as well as quenches the thirst for water. It seemed, therefore, perfect for planting coffee. Except for one thing – the inland mountains of this island, which the English called Ceylon, had never been properly cultivated. There were no roads to cart out heavy supplies. And worst of all, it was plagued by wild beasts in every shape and size – from voracious mice to rampaging elephants.

And there was one other problem the English faced. The island didn't belong to them. At least not yet.

At the turn of the 19th century, Ceylon was in the orbit of the Dutch. Before the Dutch, Portugal had used the island as a trading outpost. But both the Portuguese and the Dutch had access only to areas adjacent to the ports, rather than the more fertile regions inland. Though the Dutch attempted to grow coffee in the coastal flatlands, they were never commercially successful as the soil and altitude wasn't right for it.

Curiously, coffee was known on the island long before the European powers came there. But it wasn't primarily used as either a food or a drink, rather as an ornament by the Singhalese Buddhists

118

who found the coffee flowers exceptionally fragrant and would drape them around their temples as a kind of perfumed sacrament – a bit of information I find charming and insightful, especially as European planters and merchants regarded the coffee bean as nothing less than a vegetal form of gold. They must have been incredibly bemused at seeing those gentle Buddhists who wanted nothing more from that remarkable plant than the sweet scent of its blossoms! (Later, in England, coffee would be used as a potent disinfectant for mildew-infested homes. The power of our olfactory sense shouldn't be underestimated. Nor should we underrate the infinite variety of human imagination.)

The English were keen to plant coffee in the mountainous region that lay inland. However, this region was still in control of the Kingdom of Kandy which had been struggling over the centuries to keep its independence. Having outwitted and outmanoeuvred both the Portuguese and Dutch, the Kandyans had developed the art of guerrilla tactics and had made their villages nearly impenetrable, keeping the rugged paths of entry well hidden.

It took three wars to finally conquer Ceylon – the English and their hired mercenaries suffering serious losses. But for the English planters, winning the war was only half the battle. Before the plantations could be constructed, thousands of acres of dense forestland had to be cleared.

Writing in the mid-19th century, an English traveller spoke of his horror at the mass slaughter of elephants that, up till then, had freedom to roam but now were being sacrificed so vast plantations could be built without fear of rampaging beasties.

It took years to cut down the trees and dig out the stumps before the land was ready for planting – a job that was 'given' to native Singhalese who no longer had rights of tenure. Over the following decades a million Tamals from Southern India were brought in to till the soil. Unlike, the West Indies, slaves weren't used but the severe demands of the contract labour system meant impoverished people who worked the fields were only one step away from serfdom.

By the 1830s, decent roads had been opened up in the hill country and cultivation took place on a more extensive scale; so that in an incredibly short time the mountain ranges in the centre of the island became covered with plantations and rows of coffee trees began to bloom upon the solitary hills.

In 1864, a planter's directory for Ceylon, listed over 800 coffee estates producing, in total, nearly 70 million pounds of coffee for export back to England. Young men who had never seen a coffee tree came to Ceylon by the shipload, lured by the thought of a plot of land, easy money and good weather. Speculators took note. The price of property shot up. The Ceylonese land rush was on.

Then in 1869 something happened that changed the course of history for Ceylon and for the global coffee trade. It wasn't war. It wasn't revolution. It was, in fact, a simple fungus – Hemileia vastatrix by name – which caused something known as coffee rust, a disease so virulent that by 1884, fifteen years after the fungus was first recognised, the entire coffee industry of Ceylon lay in ruins. The coffee plantations were abandoned. All that remained was the ghostly trumpeting of elephants (until, of course, tea was planted)..

Burning coffee plantations in Haiti, 1791

❖14❖

BIRTH OF THE COFFEE REPUBLIC

BY THE 19TH century coffee was being consumed throughout Europe, but supplies were drying up. The loss of Haiti as the major source of production caused a crisis that threatened to bring many in the industry to a state of collapse. Expansion was needed, but where would it come from? As it turned out, the sleeping giant lay in the West and to the South.

Even its name came from a plant. Pau-brasil, known in English as Brazilwood, was the first commodity that helped define the massive chunk of land below the Guyanas and above Argentina. Used to dye cloth a deep, luxurious red, Brazilwood was harvested in massive quantities by European traders at the behest of an anxious textile industry.

The lands that would eventually make up the country of Brazil were claimed by Portugal at the very start of the 16th century and quickly colonised. Native tribes were vanquished, coastal forests denuded and Portugal's dispossessed peasantry brought in to exploit the terrain. Brazilwood was soon dwarfed as the chief commodity of trade by something else that was sweeter and even more profitable. That something else was sugarcane.

In many ways, sugar paved the way for coffee – both in organising techniques of mass production through the plantation system and by providing the essential resource the plantation owners thought they couldn't be without – which was African slaves. Sugar also lubricated coffee's entry into the marketplace by making a bitter substance more palatable. So the two commodities often rode in tandem, except sugar got there first.

Brazil's sugarcane cycle lasted from the first decades of the 16th century to around 1700. The massive business that Brazil established in this commodity helped build an infrastructure that would later be put to use in establishing their monumental coffee trade. But as the term 'sugarcane cycle' suggests, the economic model based on monocultures, or dependency on a single agricultural product to provide a national income, translated into a system of continual boom and bust. In the case of sugar, the plantation system first established in Brazil was easy to replicate in the new colonies that France, Holland and England set up in the Caribbean, which had the advantage of being closer to the entry ports of Europe. By the early 18th century the price of sugar had plummeted due to overexpansion and Brazil was thrown into economic crisis.

Coffee came to save the day, but its entry was slow and meandering. According to legend, in 1727 seedlings were first smuggled into the northern Brazilian province of Pará, just south of the Guyanas, by an army officer sent to negotiate a border dispute with the French. Of course by that time coffee plants were available through numerous sources but sometimes people need an apocryphal tale to help make history a little less tedious (even if less understandable). Often these fables have metaphorical undertones and in the case of this particular legend of coffee first coming to Brazil, it's wrapped around the story of a sexually frustrated wife of a French bureaucrat and a handsome Brazilian soldier who convinces her to hide a few coffee seedlings in a floral bouquet which she obligingly passes to him as a parting gift. Consequently, (according to the tale) these seedlings became the momma plants that made Brazil into a coffee empire – at the expense of the French. What this says about the relative virility of French and Luso-Brazilians and how it might relate to the fecundity of coffee plants or the nature of commodity economics in the period of late colonialism is the subject of another book. Suffice it to say that coffee came to the Pará province of Brazil sometime in the early 18th century, whether by ruse, straightforward purchasing or the emigration of planters from somewhere else, and soon spread southward as the coffee market expanded.

In 1750, a mere 12 tons of coffee was sent to Portugal from Pará. Compared to the coffee being exported from the Caribbean, this was a pittance. Even by the end of Brazil's colonial period coffee was still only a minor export commodity grown primarily in the Amazon basin. Then sometime around 1770 coffee was planted in the region of Rio de Janeiro where both soil and climate were better suited for commercial production. Within a few years, coffee plants were being grown on scattered plantations built into the hillsides of the southern hinterland. From then on the expansion of the coffee culture was very rapid, soon extending to the Sao Paulo plateau, where it eventually found its most lucrative home.

But it was the Haitian revolution in 1790s that gave real impetus to the Brazilian coffee trade. Whereas the other coffee producing countries were unable to expand production either through limitation of land or people to farm it, the sudden plunge in exports from the Caribbean provided an opening for Brazilian planters to quickly increase their holdings by carving out new plantations from virgin forests which, at that point, seemed almost limitless. Added to this, refugee planters from Haiti were invited to Brazil where they provided the expertise in coffee processing lacking in the Brazilian coffee farms that had up till then been set up without much knowledgeable guidance.

It's here that another might-have-been in the global coffee trade comes into play. In fact it was the neighbouring island of Cuba that was first to benefit from the Haitian coffee implosion. French planters from Haiti originally took refuge there and helped to organise a network of plantations based on the Haitian model. The Cuban coffee industry then grew with enormous speed and could have easily supplemented the massive shortfall caused by the destruction of the Haitian economy. But two things stood in the way – one was an act of God, the other of flesh and blood humans.

Cuba was then, as it is today, an island both blessed and cursed by nature. The land itself was perfectly suited for growing rich and robust coffee trees but the weather cycle was such that a series of fatal hurricanes destroyed a decade's worth of growth in a matter of weeks. Just as fatal, however, was the policy of retaliation imposed by the Cuban authorities against the French after the capture of the Spanish royal family by Napoleon, which forced the Haitian refugee planters to leave. Many of these French-Haitian-Cubans found a welcome home in Brazil where they joined other refugees who together became an enormous asset in helping to launch the most remarkable coffee empire the world had ever seen. Cuba, however, still grew coffee but never again as a major export – proving once more, if proof be needed, that a short-sighted immigration policy provides a blinkered nation with a knife to cut the very hand that feeds it.

The development of the Brazilian coffee industry was different from the other places where it was first commercially grown. Partly this had to do with the nature of Brazil itself and the uniqueness of the Portuguese colonial experience when compared with that of Britain, Holland, France and Spain.

Whereas the other European colonial powers developed coffee farms in places like Java where the Dutch acted as overlords and in Ceylon where the English planters were simply farming a patch of land they had expropriated through military might or in the West Indies where the French, English and Dutch took over limited, sparsely populated island territories or coastal regions which became something like overseas gardens that existed solely to supply the needs and desires of the European markets, Portuguese Brazil stood out in contrast.

By the time coffee had become a commodity of economic importance, Portugal had already been on a downward spiral as a global power from its glory days a century or so before. Unlike northern European nations that had become centres of industrial ferment, Portugal was a country of displaced peasants with few smoky factories or demon mills as a bleak but possible alternative. Thus Portugal's colonial possessions, especially in the case of Brazil, were looked upon as an opening for desperate homesteaders (something like the western parts of North America were becoming for Scandinavians, Scots and Irish). Brazil with its territorial vastness, its fertile soil and its unexploited and undeveloped resources acted as a powerful magnet to those jobless Portuguese looking for a way out of their economic quagmire. That, in itself was little different than the desires of the impoverished workers in the north of Europe. What was dissimilar, however, was the historical demographics unique to the Iberian peninsula, where African Moors, Mid-Eastern Jews and Romanised Christians stewed for centuries in the same pot, that made the peasantry of Portugal less racially sensitive than the 'whiter', of both mind and body, populations to the north.

Like Britain's vast colony in North America, the great landmass of Brazil was far too big and energetic to control from across the ocean – especially by a mother country whose power had so diminished. And, in the case of Brazil, the relative position between colony and coloniser was turned on its head in 1808 when the Portuguese court fled there after Napoleon's invasion. From the 1820s on, for all intents and purposes, Brazil was an independent state, though the official designation of 'republic' didn't come till much later in the century.

So how did this all affect coffee and the story of its globalised development? For coffee to realise its potential as a commodity of mass consumption it needed the possibility of substantial expansion to make it affordable to ordinary working people. The Caribbean colonies were limited in the amount of coffee they could grow. Besides which, colonial production was chancy – as the Haitian revolution showed. Brazil, on the other hand, was becoming an independent nation with a seemingly limitless amount of land that could be cleared for farming.

Also, coffee production up till then had been worked by either slave or indentured labour. Brazil, from the very outset, had a mixed labour force of both bonded workers and chattel slaves. Small coffee holdings were not uncommon which were often family run operations. Even though the largest and most profitable plantations were worked by slaves and even though Brazil clung to its slave trade longer than any other nation, the use of free immigrant labour increased exponentially as the century went on, allowing an alternative model of coffee production to co-exist with the traditional slave-based one. This created a more diverse coffee industry that, when the time came, had an easier transition to a non-slave labour force than the other slave-based countries.

Even more important was the fact that Brazil as an independent nation was able to mould its political decision making around the commodity that by the late 19th century was providing its main source of wealth. Coffee barons who had grown enormously rich over the years, were able to become political power brokers in a way that was impossible in the colonial coffee producing world. Thus the coffee trade was supported in Brazil through government financing of roads, rails and collateral industries. More crucially, enormous subsidies were given directly to the coffee growers when overproduction threatened to bring the entire business crashing down.

But similar to what happened with its sugar industry, Brazil's dependency on a single agricultural commodity meant trouble. As we shall see later, the Coffee Republic was actually built on a shaky house of cards.

Jean d'Ylen, 1928

❖15❖

Coffee comes of age

UP UNTIL THE middle of the 19th century coffee was usually purchased green and roasted in the home. Shops hadn't yet taken on the character we're familiar with now – as the purveyor of packaged goods. Everything for sale was either in enormous jars, Hessian sacks or great wooden barrels. For consumers of coffee, both in Europe and North America, beans were usually sold out of the bags they had been shipped in.

Early on, coffeehouses themselves provided the retail service of selling beans directly to householders. Later, people would purchase their coffee supplies from market stalls and peddlers on a haphazard basis, depending on what was available at the time. Though coffee drinkers were expected to roast and grind their own beans, it was possible to purchase 'coffee powder' from either a coffeehouse or market stall. Roasted coffee beans were often pulverised by mortar and pestle as grinding equipment was still in short supply. As a matter of fact, some coffee connoisseurs still prefer that method.

In the home, coffee was roasted in long handled pans over wood or charcoal fires. The process, of getting an even roast, required a modicum of skill but the result was worth the trouble, especially when good quality coffee beans had been acquired. The problem was that coffee beans were often delivered in poor condition. It took many years before proper shipping techniques could be enforced. When first transported from the East Indies, coffee was often used as ballast and the taste was influenced by whatever else had been shipped alongside it – which could well have been pepper. But as the market progressed, suitable shipping and storage techniques were better understood and precautions were taken to prevent mildew and other damage that would affect the taste of even the best coffee beans.

Of course it took a while before people's palates were sophisticated enough to know what good coffee tasted like. The early coffeehouses mainly served pretty vile stuff cooked in boiling cauldrons where taste was definitely secondary to the required effect. Outside of England and North America, there was more regard for brewing techniques that could get the best out of whatever coffee was on offer. By the late 18th century quite a few books had been published as guides to coffee preparation and a number of exotic brewing devices were being experimented with.

Coffee's journey to prominence wasn't always an easy ride however. Throughout the 18th and 19th century there were competing interests that saw the coffee trade as a nuisance, hindrance or intruder into previously claimed territory within the world of beverage consumption. First among these outraged interests was the beer industry, represented by tavern owners who feared their business was being affected by the bright beckoning lights of the coffee cafés. To protect their turf they were not averse to using underhanded tactics like writing up false reports on the negative health effects of drinking coffee. It caused impotence, they claimed, whereas beer made men virile. One of these early attempts at besmirching the coffee drink was an infamous petition said to be initiated by a group of housewives who claimed that coffee was a 'drying enfeebling liquor'. Was there a better way of getting men to prick up their ears?

Besides the beer lobby, there were other forces opposed to the importation of this foreign substance into European lands. In the early 18th century, the ideas of mercantilism still dominated the economics of most western governments. Germany and Sweden, for example, thought coffee was a threat to their national wealth as it was imported from countries that were colonised by competing European powers, consequently affecting their balance of trade. In 1780 Prussian coffee sniffers were said to have searched people's houses to make sure they weren't grinding beans illegally as all coffee was to be purchased through government run shops. A well-known lithograph – satirical, perhaps – was based on the outrage German coffee lovers felt towards the incredible idea of trying to restrict coffee consumption by banning its domestic use, an absurd policy that was soon rescinded. But high tariffs and import duties would have been more effective if not for porous borders that made smuggling a lucrative trade.

The urban landscape changed dramatically from the mid-19th century onwards, in accordance with a major shift in purchasing habits. Wages and salaries increased to a point where families had more of an expendable income, while, at the same time, the culture of self-sufficiency where bread would be baked and clothes would be sewn and morning coffee roasted by the women at home, was starting to break down. The factory society was rapidly creating a culture of mass production that required an equivalent culture of mass consumption so that production could be further increased (ad infinitum).

As part of this process, main streets and high roads were transformed both in appearance and purpose. The covered markets were replaced by specialty shops which catered to ordinary folk as well as the middle classes. Unlike earlier times, bulk goods were now packaged on the spot and sold at a fixed price for ready cash. As a result, coffee became accessible to a wider population at an affordable price as imports from the various producing countries continued to grow. What's more, from the mid-19th century, grocers gave customers the option of purchasing their coffee pre-roasted and ground rather than buying green and roasting beans themselves.

What's remarkable is how late this ability to buy pre-roasted coffee in a grocery store came about. And it wasn't an easy sell. After all, people who were used to roasting their own saw no good reason for paying more money to purchase beans that were already roasted and ground, as both the taste and quality were bound to suffer. Yet for the great majority of people who had neither the time nor patience to go through that particular morning ritual, the ability to buy coffee ready-to-brew meant the consumption figures would skyrocket.

The transformation in coffee sales and distribution that began in the mid-1800s was nearly complete at the century's end. By that time the rail networks were essentially in place, shipping had gone from sail to steam and high street shops had decidedly taken over from the markets and fairs. By the early twentieth century, purpose built warehouses provided safe storage for imported coffee beans which were processed by industrial roasters, packaged and then sent out into the retail chain. But few people woke up to the fragrant smell of roasting coffee and fresh baked scones any longer, most preferring instead factory-made loaves and packaged, pre-ground coffee soon to go stale, mollified only by spoonfuls of sugar and dollops of cream. Could this have been progress? I wonder...

The issue of progress is a dicey one and often cuts a number of ways. When ordinary people were poor and bound to get poorer and the world was such that only a very small sector of the population could afford to buy coffee – real coffee, at any rate – two things followed: firstly, coffee production was frozen by limited demand and secondly, the vast majority of the world's population were denied the beauty and excitement of a good coffee buzz.

Limited demand coupled with limited supply, of course, meant coffee was expensive. One way around the conundrum of expanding the number of coffee drinkers while imports were low and coffee pricey was by the age-old trick of watering down the brew. A teaspoon of coffee grounds could provide one cup or two, depending on the strength of the essence required. The early coffeehouses were not averse to adjusting the brew to fit the cost of beans – stronger when beans were cheap, weaker when they were expensive.

Another method of artificial price control, which also expanded the supply, was through adulteration. A number of different vegetables and grains were used to provide bulk to coffee grounds, thus lowering the price per pound while increasing the pounds on offer. Sometimes this was surreptitious, sometimes done quite openly – as with chicory, which was said to have been developed as a coffee substitute during the time of the continental blockade in 1807.

But carrots and turnips, roasted till they were charred and caramelised, often were used as well.

I remember as a youth spending some time in New Orleans which had developed a taste for chicory during the Napoleonic era and still used it as an additive to make café Louisiane. The coffee brewed was viscous as treacle – you almost had to cut it with a knife and eat it with a spoon. But people there loved it so much that a clever food manufacturer developed a national brand of chicory-polluted coffee, geared, I suppose to Louisiana expats living in other parts of America as well as those tourists who went to New Orleans and, for some strange reason, wanted to capture a bit of the flavour they had innocently stumbled upon – rather like travellers from the US bringing back Marmite they had naively ingested in England.

Coffee is one of those special commodities that has a certain amount of price inelasticity. Unlike things that people only buy when they have money to burn, coffee is looked upon by its habitual users as a necessity – something they couldn't (or wouldn't) easily do without. Some wealthier consumers, therefore, would continue to buy coffee at almost any price (as they do today at the more outrageous coffee emporiums). So, once established, coffee had a guaranteed market, even if limited. From the trader's point of view, the only question was how to expand it.

137

The eventual extension of the coffee trade came from push by producers and pull by the traders. It was also helped along by the idea of Brazil and the notion of the independent coffee state. Colonial coffee could be controlled by the mother country either through taxation or political command, where both were used as levers to keep the price of coffee high but relatively stable. It was more difficult to manage the output of a country like Brazil that saw progress in terms of increased coffee production no matter what and thus took measures which made it possible for their growers to survive even when prices were plummeting because of oversupply and under demand.

But ultimately coffee production needed to be balanced by sales in the coffee consuming nations. Increased sales, however, were harder to generate prior to the onset of mass media. In the 19th and early 20th centuries, advertising as we know it today existed only in a very rudimentary form. Even though there was a multitude of newspapers and magazines, the base readership was actually quite small until well into the 20th century.

Of course there were always ways of 'getting the message across,' mainly having to do with visual art such as posters and wall paintings – and, later, window displays and clever promotional packaging. Better still was by word of mouth (as it probably is today). That, however, depended on establishing areas of mutual interest that went beyond class divides – something that was easier to accomplish in the new world than the old one.

In the end, coffee sold itself through the dynamic coffeehouse culture that developed with such vitality in Europe and America. Coffee had also become an integral part of people's domestic life. They enjoyed lingering over a cup and found that after a second they were suddenly capable of saying things that seemed extraordinarily brilliant – a nice way to start the day that would inevitably become less inspired unless a third cup was on offer (and possibly even a fourth).

So coffee was there, people liked it and it wasn't going away. In fact, by the mid-1800s, coffee had become so popular that it was being grown throughout the tropics in a belt that spanned the globe which came to be known as 'the coffee zone'.

Early American Coffee Roasting Factory

❖16❖

THE COLOSSUS OF THE NORTH

JUST AS THE Brazilian coffee republic – the Colossus of the South – became paramount in coffee production, dwarfing all other coffee growers by dint of its enormous size and unlimited harvests, the United States of America – the Colossus of the North – became the major country of consumption fuelling this expansion.

The coffee culture had spread to North America very early on by colonists, already familiar with the brew, who brought the habit with them from Europe. Before coffee was grown in the Caribbean, however, the cost of beans was dreadfully expensive for Americans who could only obtain Ottoman or Indonesian coffee that had been trans-shipped from Amsterdam or London. But once it was grown on what were essentially offshore islands, like Haiti, Cuba and Puerto Rico, coffee became both cheaper and readily available.

There is a pervasive myth that the consumption of coffee in the United States was somehow a patriotic decision based on English taxation policies prior to the colonial revolution. The Boston Tea Party (the symbolism of which has become rampant in recent years) is often mentioned as a key event that led to colonial distaste for Chinese grown infusions. The fact that Canadians also seemed to prefer coffee even though they remained loyal to the King, is neatly avoided. As one European traveller observed after touring the Canadian provinces in the late 1700s, people drank coffee but hardly ever tea. He put it down, quite rightly, not to a particular distaste for tea but rather to China being far away and the Caribbean being near.

Another thing to consider when making grandiose statements that homogenize the predilections of early North Americans, is that even in the 18th century the territory that was patched together to eventually form the United States was populated by people from various cultural and linguistic backgrounds – along with the British there were also Dutch, German, French, Spanish, Portuguese, Scandinavian and Native Americans. In fact Pennsylvania, the home of the 'Liberty Bell', was equally divided between English and German speakers at the time of the revolution whose culinary and drinking habits were as different as their notions of what a future Republic might actually look like (to say nothing of the black Africans who made up a sizeable chunk of the population in 1776 and weren't consulted as to the proposed Bill of Rights or whether they preferred having coffee or tea with their meals).

That being said, the various populations of North America did seem to like coffee and consumed it in vast quantities at numerous establishments – very much based on the European coffeehouse models – as well as in the privacy of their homes.

A quick look at a map of North America in the 18th century would show how many routes coffee could have taken from the nearest plantation zones. The territories that France maintained till the early 1800s, Louisiana and onwards up along the Mississippi River into Canada, would have had coffee shipped directly from Haiti. The Spanish possession of Florida was only 90 miles from the coffee plantations in Cuba. (The Seminole Indians of Florida were known to trade furs and honey with the Spanish in exchange for coffee and tobacco.) And the western territories had an easy supply line through Mexico, which was an exporter of coffee from the Antilles until it started growing its own.

Also, quite a few colonists from the Caribbean eventually made their way to the mainland. Though coffee never became a commercial crop in the territories that would become the United States, the coffee culture came with them. After the Haitian revolution of the 1790s, a number of French coffee planters were offered refuge in Pennsylvania (of all places!). What they did there is anyone's guess, but it's likely that their coffee connections were put to some use or other.

However, it probably was the European refugees from the revolutions of 1848 that did most to establish a vital café culture in the United States. These were mainly urbanised, middle-class intellectuals, many of whom had learned the cut and thrust of radical discourse in the coffeehouses of Berlin, Vienna,

Prague and Budapest. For many of them, cafés were a way of life that they easily transferred to their new homeland.

By the late 19th century, coffee had become king in the energised, post-revolutionary world that was the United States of America. A glance at the statistics collected by Francis Thurber for *The American Grocer* in the 1880s, indicates what an extraordinary amount of coffee was being consumed in North America by then. The two main ports of entry into the US at that time were New York, where coffee arrived from Brazil, and San Francisco, which received coffee from Central America. From 1878 to 1880, New York took in an average of 264 million pounds per year of Brazilian beans; San Francisco received an average of 17 million pounds over the same period, mainly from Guatemala, Costa Rica, El Salvador and Nicaragua.

As a whole, over that period of time, the United States consumed a yearly amount of 345 million pounds of coffee. In contrast, the average annual consumption Thurber gave for European countries was: Germany – 224 million pounds; France – 119 million pounds; Austria – 81 million pounds; Netherlands – 68 million pounds; Belgium – 48 million pounds; United Kingdom – 33 million pounds; Italy – 28 million pounds; Spain and Portugal combined – only 7 million pounds.

These statistics need to be looked at with a certain amount of scepticism as there were a number of issues that could have easily skewed the numbers. As mentioned before, smuggling back then was so common and extensive that it was hardly seen as a criminal act except by the tax authorities. Also, imports into places like Hamburg and Amsterdam were often processed and re-exported to other countries, so realistic data on domestic consumption is often hard to determine. Even so, the figures do give an idea of the relative spread of coffee in the late 19th century and show how dominant the United States was in the list of consumer nations.

Thurber's book entitled *Coffee From Plantation to Cup*, written in 1884, was one of the first in the English language to approach the economic and social history of coffee from a North American perspective. His interest was clearly motivated through love of the bean and a fascination with its story. There's even a charming dedication to a coffee vendor at the Poughkeepsie rail station. 'I do not know his name,' wrote Thurber, 'but year in and year out he gives the public an ideal cup of coffee...' (He then went on to complain about the dire state of coffee vending in America.)

But Thurber was also a businessman, beholden to the coffee industry which was now going full throttle several decades after the Civil War. His book, chock full of statistical data and analysis, was part of a growing trend to rationalise industry by applying new scientific principles that demanded technicians schooled in the art of number crunching.

The 19th century coffee industry, now firmly rooted in North America, was energising the new political and economic order as well as being energised by it. The rapid industrialisation of both the United States and Northern Europe provided the tools for the next leap forward on the road toward mass consumption.

Technology that transformed the coffee trade had been in the works for quite a while and was often based on equipment developed for multiple uses – like the steam engine. Various countries seemed to focus on certain aspects of coffee technology that fit its national character – France, a country obsessed with food, became fascinated with new systems of gourmet brewing while Germany, which vied with England for engineering prominence, had established a lead in global sales of roasting equipment. Each month, it seemed, new patents were being issued on a variety of devices and equipment that would either brew a better cup or help industrialise coffee's production, allowing for a vastly increased market that had barely been tapped till then.

But it was in the United States that all the new technologies and coffee paraphernalia were put to the test. In cities throughout the country, small roasteries that had been set up in neighbourhoods to provide fresh coffee for local shops were soon to be replaced by smoke-belching factories that would roast, blend, grind, package and distribute a standardised coffee product, easily purchased and consumed by a vast new market beyond the urban centres.

The industrialisation of coffee production and distribution didn't happen all at once. As with all transformations, conditions needed to be right before what was going to happen actually did. But once things fell into place, the shift from localised, artisanal facilities to industrial-scale enterprise with national distribution took place with great rapidity.

One example of how this came about is through the story of a small San Francisco company that was established around the time of the California Gold Rush. Pioneer Steam Coffee and Spice Mills started out by supplying coffee and condiments to the thousands of immigrant miners who were descending on the city and clogging the ports with abandoned ships to such an extent that some of them had to be torched and sunk in order to make room for vital cargo vessels. But the city was growing so fast (from a little over 200 residents in 1848 to about 36,000 six years later) that quite soon this tiny coffee supplier was forced to expand its operations.

At first the company had very limited facilities, using hand-cranked machinery for roasting and grinding, but in order to supply the miners who were heading out to the Sierra gold fields, they began packing ground coffee into tins, selling them by the caseload to anxious would-be prospectors who used the brew not only as a stimulant but as a way to stave off hunger. Very soon demand was so great that the company relocated, expanding their size exponentially and upgrading their machinery to the latest steam-powered equipment. By 1855 they were distributing huge quantities of their packaged coffee throughout the region. In a few decades more they had become a national brand – Folgers – selling packaged coffee in grocery stores everywhere that had running water and a train station.

This sort of story was replicated all over the United States in the 19th century, though perhaps not in such a dramatic manner. Another glimpse into the incredible speed of change in the coffee business can be witnessed through the tale of Joel Owsley Cheek, a resident of Nashville, Tennessee, who died in 1935 at the age of 83.

I can do no better than to quote from this little gem of an obituary: 'Mr Cheek's first job was as a salesman with a Nashville wholesale grocery house at $50 a month ... In those days coffee was sold "green" and the roasting was done in home ovens. Cheek started roasting it on a small scale and in 1898 formed a company to exploit his product which he had named for a hotel, Maxwell House, noted as a gathering place for southern political and social leaders ... In 1928 the Cheek-Neal Coffee company was sold for approximately $40,000,000...'

The period after the US Civil War, was known as the Gilded Age (an ironic term coined by the 19th century satirist, Mark Twain). It was a time of enormous economic growth spurred on both by national reconstruction after years of devastating military conflict and by the completion in 1869 of the transcontinental railway that allowed goods to be shipped to the western territories in a matter of days rather than months.

Coffee's industrialization in the United States coincided with this period of rapid expansion and was first launched by individuals from ordinary backgrounds who learned their trade at the coalface and could see the future opportunities that existed by marketing coffee in a more consumer friendly manner – as well as taking advantage of the frenzied movement west of many thousands of workers descending on the Pacific states without, as yet, an adequate infrastructure to supply them.

What these early entrepreneurs all had in common was a certain amount of business acumen, access to a network of retailers and the ability to find ready money necessary for capital expenditures which allowed them to lay the groundwork for a national distribution of packaged, pre-roasted coffee sold in grocer's shops.

In North American mythology, this process was known as the 'Horatio Alger effect' – a syndrome having at its core the abiding principle that hard work coupled with bright ideas necessarily brought its just reward of enormous wealth. Anyone, the story went, no matter from what background (as long as they possessed the right epidermal pigmentation), could make it in America if they were willing to work hard and do whatever it took to mosey down that golden pathway to success.

Actually, this particular dream did seem to come true for a certain number of the chosen few – up to a point, that is, and as long as one ignored the many who tried to build their own little coffee empires and lost everything in the process. However, those who succeeded did so either as part of (or in spite of) the internecine company warfare that was waged whereby the big became bigger, the strong became stronger while the small struggled to survive.

We can see this played out in the stories of two families that came to loggerheads at the end of the century – culminating in an extended period of brutal conflict that was eventually documented in the proceedings of the New York State Legislature's investigation of trusts in 1897.

John Arbuckle was the son of Scottish immigrants who worked for his family's wholesale grocery business in Pittsburgh. Sometime in the 1860s he developed a process of coating green coffee beans with a gelatinous mixture of sugar and eggs as a preservative – a supposed way of keeping roasted coffee beans fresh after weeks of transport and storage.

The coffee processing and distribution business that Arbuckle and his brother set up invested heavily in technology which enabled them to package roasted coffee in small paper bags, which were hermetically sealed and labelled. Using unique marketing devices for the time, the coffee packets were sold mainly to grocers in the West under the name of 'Ariosa'.

By 1891 Ariosa coffee was the top selling brand in the United States. But in order to keep his production costs down while continuing to coat the beans with his patented preservative, Arbuckle needed to purchase large quantities of sugar at a rock-bottom price.

This is where the second family comes into the picture. The Havemeyers were German immigrants who came to New York early in the 18th century and set up a company that grew to become the major sugar production operation in North America. By the mid-1800s, the American Sugar Refining Company, which the family owned, was the dominant force in what became known as the Sugar Trust – a quasi-legal monopoly that controlled sugar pricing and distribution throughout the country.

Finding it impossible to acquire sugar at competitive prices through available sources, the Arbuckles decided to open a sugar refinery of their own. In response, the Havemeyers went into the coffee business with the sole purpose of punishing the upstart Arbuckles. To this end, in 1896 the

Havemeyers, along with their cohorts in the Sugar Trust, bought control of an Ohio coffee roastery, the Woolson Spice Company, for 2 million dollars – an enormous sum when compared to what the money of that period would be worth today.

The Havemeyers then promoted the Woolson Spice Company's Lion Coffee brand through an unparalleled mass-marketing campaign, attempting to undercut Arbuckle's Ariosa trade by pricing Lion Coffee at a loss in order to force the Arbuckles into an economic war of attrition.

However, fortunately for the Arbuckles, this trade war was being played out during a period of growing electoral opposition to the crass audacity of the very wealthy company overlords who were becoming collectively known in popular parlance as 'Robber Barons' due to their high-handed practices – which included brazenly buying government influence, paying dirt cheap wages to their workers and crushing competition by any means necessary.

The New York State Legislative Committee to Investigate Trusts met in the beginning of February, 1897 looking into the dealings of the Havemeyer's American Sugar Refining Company. However, while investigating one trust the committee gained information that led them to suspect the existence of another. Thus they were sidetracked into examining the US coffee trade.

Havemeyer had testified that there were good profits in the coffee business and claimed that was the only reason his company went into it. Arbuckle, however, told the committee that ever since the Havemeyers went into the coffee business there was no profit in it any longer. He testified that the Havemeyers must be losing from $500 to $1000 a day.

Arbuckle went on to tell the committee that the Havemeyers said their coffee packages contained a blend of Java, Mocha and Rio coffees yet sold this mixture for 13 cents a pound. 'Mocha and Java,' Arbuckle told them, 'cost 21 cents each and Rio costs nearly 10 cents. We sell our coffee at 13 cents a pound and it has no Java or Mocha in it, yet we can make nothing out of the business now.' Therefore, competition with the Havemeyers meant doing business at a loss, he said.

Least we assume this was some sort of David meets Goliath event, I must stress that it definitely wasn't. By the time of the Committee's investigation, the Arbuckles had long since left the world of small but honest coffee traders. In fact, they had become every bit as big and brutal as the Havemeyers, with enormous warehouses in Brazil where coffee was stored when harvests were good and held off the market till the price rose again to be delivered by a fleet of ships owned by Arbuckle enterprises and processed in Arbuckle plants that roasted more than half the coffee consumed in North America.

A sidebar in the *New York Times* of the day summed it up nicely, putting the story in perspective of the consumer: 'One effect of the war now waging between the Arbuckles and the Sugar Trust has been the placing on sale of the so-called "package coffee." Hitherto, the sale of this had been confined almost entirely to the West, but it is now offered in this city and Brooklyn. Grocers look with disgust on this innovation, fearing that their sales of high-grade coffees will be interfered with. As the New York public has always demanded a superior article, there will doubtless be difficulty in securing any widespread sale of the package coffee here.'

Continuing on, the Times journalist concluded: 'A well-known jobber, speaking of this new feature of the coffee trade said, "The general standard of package coffee as offered to the public at present is a coffee roast in the bean, put up in an attractive paper package with a special brand printed thereon. After the brand is fully established and a demand created, through the offerings of prizes, gifts etc, the buyer will often find, if he carefully investigates, that he is paying a good price for the gifts and the brand and getting poor coffee. The grade today of the package coffee most largely sold throughout the United States could be sold by any wholesale roaster with a fair margin of profit at 12 to 12.5 cents a pound roasted. In many parts of the country the prejudice against package coffee has become so strong that the retailer destroys the wrapper and

153

mixes the coffee with better grades in order to give his customer goods at a low price and yet of improved quality."'

So there we have it. Coffee in the US had become cheap and easily marketable through new methods of industrial production and ease of distribution – but at what price to the consumer? Cities like New York held out, of course, preferring to maintain their coffee habits. Some places, though, had no choice in what kind of coffee they purchased for consumption.

It was a bad state of affairs for coffee drinkers. But it was going to get a lot worse before it got better.

❖17❖

CAFÉS OF THE BELLE EPOQUE

THE LATE 19TH century saw a flowering of café culture throughout Europe but most especially in France, Germany and Austro-Hungary. This happened in conjunction with the industrial transformation that stimulated a modernisation of the city landscape by a new class of wealthy merchants and entrepreneurs. In both Western and Central Europe, the urban metropolis was being re-imagined and redesigned, sometimes brutally, sometimes with a velvet glove, as a showcase for the affluent. Paris, Berlin, Prague, Budapest and Vienna were all revamped, rebuilt and repaved. Narrow, rat-infested alleys were replaced by magnificent boulevards lined with grandiose cafés, each one more resplendent than the next (though the new, pseudo-classical architecture was seen by some as more of a testament to the fragility of empire than serious homage to the Greco-Roman styles they tried to emulate).

But there was another side to this massive urban renewal project that laid waste to centuries of workers' housing and ancient settlements. Though airier and more sanitised, there were those who saw something frighteningly antiseptic about all the stiffly straight avenues that radiated from flawless roundabouts like the wheel spokes of a military juggernaut.

If the 'Belle Epoque' gloried in the nouveau riche, there was a counter movement as well. A massive influx of peoples had flooded through the city gates into these new, dynamic worlds bringing with them many different ways of seeing. The fabulous wealth produced by the vast industrial projects that had been launched in the mad dash to the century's end, created a world that was filled with both delight and danger. It might have been the bourgeoisie who planned the new metropolis, but it was the workers who built it – and that was something the builders weren't about to let their apparent masters easily forget.

Many fantasies were played out over this time and cafés became the place in which to play them. With the gentrification of city life came a flowering of the arts – young men (and some young women) aspired to sup with the gods on terms they defined for themselves. The café, in all its many guises, became their rendezvous.

It was especially in the cities of the short lived Austro-Hungarian Empire – Vienna, Budapest, Prague – where cafés played a vital role of bringing together the multicultural phantasmagoria that came with the many and various peoples drawn from the steppes of Crimea, Ruthenia, Moravia, Bosnia and the Ukraine. We tend to focus on the cafés that certain well-known artists and writers frequented but these weren't necessarily the places where the energy buzzed back then. Nowadays these cafés are simply museums that are visited primarily for nostalgia but during their glory days they were home to ordinary folk who might have aspired to fly or not but came there to soak up the vitality and intellectual vigour fuelled by endless cups of caffeine.

As Georges Mikes commented in his splendid introduction to a photographic tour entitled *The Coffeehouses of Europe*, the Central European coffeehouse wasn't merely a place; it was a way of life:

'Every profession used to have its own coffeehouse and its *stammtisch*, the regular table of regular guests. Every shade, faction or sub-group of each profession had its own coffeehouse... In addition to the well-known tables of artists, there were coffeehouses for textile merchants, dentists, horse-dealers, politicians and pickpockets among many others. The world of criminals was as much subdivided as every other sphere. A mere pickpocket would not be accepted by the table of self-respecting safe-breakers any more than a small money-lender would be tolerated at the table of top bankers...'

In a Viennese coffeehouse, according to Mikes, there were twenty-eight varieties of coffee drinks. The customer had a choice of a small, medium or large cup; served strong or weak, short or long depending on the amount of water added; in a glass, or in a little copper pot, with or without milk or even whipped cream. The descriptive vocabulary for coffee drinks was splendidly rich, including terms like 'Kapuziner', a reference to the dark cassock worn by Capuchin friars.

Mikes found it surprising that the Central European coffeehouse should have developed first in Vienna and not in Hungary as Hungary had been part of the Ottoman Empire for so long. The Magyar peasants, though, were never integrated into the Turkish culture and, in fact, watched the Turks drink coffee at the end of each meal with bemusement. There is a saying in the Hungarian language – 'The black soup is yet to come,' which Mikes claims was a reference to the Turks' 'masochistic habit of inflicting the punishment of black coffee on themselves.'

Yet one would hardly guess that was the case (if, indeed, it was) seeing the subsequent cafés of Budapest and the enduring relationship with coffee that accompanied the Hungarian diaspora. Indeed, when I was living in London back in the early 1970s, one of my favourite cafés was a marvellous place in South End Green which was a hangout for chess obsessed Hungarian refugees who lingered over their endless coffee while pondering some brilliant Budapest gambit. And I remember one of the regulars telling me that it took nothing more than a chessboard, a cup of freshly brewed coffee and a smoky café to make any displaced Hungarian feel at home.

Whereas in Vienna and Budapest the coffeehouse was primarily for consumption of the coffee drink in all its myriad of forms, the cafés of Paris were based around alcohol with coffee as an expected supplement. The great age of Parisian bohemia had as much to do with the ingestion of brandy and absinthe as caffeine; which is not to say that coffee wasn't taken seriously by the high-strung artists and writers who made certain cafés their home. In fact, there's a lovely story that Henri Murger relates in his roman à clef, *Scènes de la vie de bohème*, where the proprietor of the Momus Café, at the end of his tether after having been pushed to the razor's edge by the antics of his rag-tag clientele, pleads with them to desist from making their own coffee on a portable burner they had shamelessly brought into his establishment under the pretence of his coffee having been doctored with chicory. (As if to emphasise his fascination with coffee and its stimulating nature, Murger also has one of his bohemian characters whisper seductively into the ear of his friend's young wife, 'Madame, the coffee plant is a native of Arabia, where it was discovered by a goat. Its use expanded to Europe. Voltaire used to drink seventy cups a day. I like mine without sugar, but very hot.')

The smaller workers' cafés stood out in stark contrast to the grand cafés whose well-dressed clientele displayed themselves like haughty peacocks bathed in gas-lit celebrity. There the high and mighty, along with the not-so-mighty boulevardiers, gathered to see and be seen by others who were part of that puffed-up parade – or those who wished to be – in an unbridled voyeuristic ritual.

Here tuxedoed waiters ruled the roost, every bit as haughty as those they served. Out of the limelight, though, were the thousands of little places where the everyday people of Paris collected for their morning coffee and brioche. Usually family-run operations, these workers' cafés popped up on almost every street, providing a safe and cosy space to read and write and gossip and explore; each of these cafés establishing its own personality along with its unique clientele.

In post–Haussmann Paris, rich and poor lived cheek by jowl in a vertical arrangement that had the bourgeoisie inhabiting the ground floor of apartment blocks where each succeeding level had a lowering of social status with the attic reserved for the most hungry and destitute. This, of course, was when stairways were the only method of ascending to the upper storeys, so gout-ridden bankers were quite happy to forgo viewing the beauty of a Parisian skyline in exchange for easy access (even if later generations would have it just the other way, with the rich above and the poor below – which they saw as more in line with the natural order of the cosmos). What that meant was quartiers or neighbourhoods were fairly mixed as far as social class and occupation. Local cafés often reflected this diversity.

In contrast to the coffeehouses of Central Europe, the drink served up in Paris cafés was usually quite straightforward (even if the beans, as Murger hinted, were often mixed with grain or chicory). Coffee was served either black or white without any pretence. But morning coffee had become a defining part of the culture – so much so that the impressionists, who frequented the cafés in the unpaved streets of Montmartre, made stylised portraits of coffee paraphernalia almost into a genre.

Parisian bohemia at the fin de siecle created a mythology of paint splattered canvasses exchanged for coffee and brandy by dirt-poor artists living one day to the next at the behest of kind-hearted patrons who subsidised their drinking habits. How often this actually happened is neither here nor there as the image is, in fact, what counts in fuelling one's historical imagination. But for generations of youthful artists who consumed these stories about the 19th century gallery of greats staining their smocks with coffee along with colourful oils, the fantasy of the bohemian cafés as adjuncts to their cramped studios and workplaces redolent with the scent of coffee and tobacco, is what matters. Many have sought them out only to find they existed in the realm of fanciful legend. But once established, the romance of the Parisian café with its dark roasted coffee in a white porcelain cup exciting the bristles of an artist's brush persists as a compelling vision that beckons through the mist of timelessness.

Parisian Café, Gaetano de Las Heras 1903

❖18❖

COFFEE AND THE TEMPERANCE MOVEMENT

I BECAME INTERESTED in the Temperance Movement because England, at a certain time, was accused of being a tea-drinking nation and I wasn't sure this was the case. It may have been true on a statistical level when consumption was averaged out, but such preferences ebbed and flowed over the years. Certainly, after the collapse of Ceylon as England's major coffee supplier, when the plantations had switched over to growing tea, there was a push for home consumption of the leaf rather than the bean.

However, Robert Montgomery Martin in his book, *The Past and Present State of the Tea Trade of England*, published in 1838, refers to the numerous coffeehouses still active in London, stating that there were '3,000 of these highly useful establishments in the metropolis, in which are daily consumed 2,000 pounds of tea, and 15,000 pounds of coffee' – not an insignificant amount and an increase from several years before, which Martin suggests was due to the growing Temperance movement.

In fact, over the course of the 19th century coffee consumption had spread throughout most urban areas in the United Kingdom with the market having been re-energised by a buoyant prohibitionist campaign that promoted the 'coffee tavern' as a substitute for alcohol driven bars and pubs. Though the coffee taverns – as they were called in deference to the pub-drinking working-class culture – were a relatively short-lived phenomenon, they helped to establish coffee as a drink in areas where it hadn't been consumed before.

Much money and organisation went into building, sponsoring and running these alcohol free ventures that hoped to provide a safe and communal space for the British working class to sober up. However, the problem with the early temperance movement and its relationship with the working classes was that by and large it looked to be just another creature of cosy, well off and cosseted social reformers. Even though the temperance cause was later taken up by certain groups of workers – including, for a time, socialists who viewed alcoholism as an enemy of the people – in the main it was used by the staunch upholders of Victorian values as a way of lending moral guidance to their lessers.

An extraordinary little document entitled 'Practical hints on Management of Coffee Taverns' was published in 1878 by an organisation calling itself The Coffee Tavern Company, Ltd. In a brief introduction, the authors claimed its purpose was 'to furnish the many people who are anxious to see Coffee Taverns established in their neighbourhood, some information as to the sort of thing that a Coffee Tavern is and the conditions on which it can be made successful.'

At the time this pamphlet was published, British industry was still struggling to attain a temperate labour force that could come to work on time, bright and sober – especially on Monday mornings when, traditionally, the agricultural labourers of past decades (soon to be the urban proletariat) could take time off to recuperate from Sunday frivolities when more than a few thirsty pints would be happily quaffed.

According to this little how-to guide, the basis of the coffee tavern movement was to give an alternative place for the labouring classes to go after their work was over – somewhere they could stay sober rather than losing themselves in the alcoholic haze of a boozy pub. The attempt by the temperance movement to either close down the alcohol-based taverns or, at the very least, severely limit the hours of operation, directly affected the working-class as often men would go there simply because they provided a warm and friendly sanctuary from their dark and dingy living quarters. So the coffee tavern was seen, by teetotallers at least, as a viable substitute.

The list of objectives given in the 1878 pamphlet is revealing. They include: the checking of intemperance by the opening of a public house in which no malt or alcoholic liquor will be sold; the satisfaction of want by a supply of cheap and wholesome food; the provision of evening recreation in free public rooms; and the consequent improvement and elevation of the national character.

It was this last objective that is most interesting and probably placed there for purposes of obtaining government and institutional support by portraying coffee taverns as a noble venture. The authors follow on by emphasising that 'persons who are directly interested in the propagation of Temperance' could rest assured that the coffee tavern provided the solution to the problem of 'frequency of relapse' when the 'convert' was deprived of his old haunt without another being substituted for it. This, they argued, 'would no longer be feared where the Coffee Tavern is properly opened and managed.'

The authors then went on to discuss where a proposed coffee tavern should be situated, suggesting that a thoroughfare with a good amount of traffic be chosen – someplace near a large factory or other place of business where many are employed. The perceived customer, they explained, likes contrast, and as his own home is often desolate, he appreciates the brightness and bustle of a public setting.

Furthermore, they advised, the tavern should have space set aside for meeting rooms and special attractions such as music. In the principal rooms, they suggested that 'newspapers should be provided in sufficient abundance, and tobacco should be lawful everywhere.' And they concluded by emphasising that, beyond all other things, what was most important to the ordinary customer was a sense of freedom and independence; stating, 'unless he makes himself particularly offensive to his neighbours, he should not be interfered with.'

Many workers, however, were suspicious of the temperance movement and their offerings which they believed were hypocritical because of the implication that the problem of drunkenness lay only with the labouring classes. They felt that middle-class social reformers constantly accused them of having created their own miseries by throwing away money on drink – a charge that only diverted attention from the real problems of poor sanitation, overcrowding, and miserable working conditions.

However, the eventual failure of the coffee taverns lay mainly with the fallacious idea that they could be imposed from above on the working-classes by a gentrified Temperance Movement whose leaders often perceived those they wished to 'help' as little more than recalcitrant children. Even though the organisers tried to model their coffee taverns on the indigenous places of leisure – the alcohol-based pubs – that had been part and parcel of ordinary neighbourhood life, they did so in such a patronizing manner that antagonisms were bound to fester amongst those many workers who had a strong sense of independence and pride and who simply wanted a place to relax and imbibe without any moral baggage being heaped on them.

Some years ago I wrote an article about the social history of coffeehouses in London for *Café Magazine*, in which I said: 'A rather artificial attempt at the recreation of a lively coffeehouse scene was made by the temperance movement in the 1880s. Modelled after the spacious, light, mahogany-trimmed taverns being promoted by the beer industry, the late Victorian coffeehouse was a conscious attempt by naive social reformers to lure the workers from their pubs and the perils of demon gin... Accordingly, customers were encouraged to bring their own food to be cooked free of charge in the tavern's kitchen; newspapers and games were laid out – also gratis – and customers were allowed to remain as long as they wanted. Needless to say, none of these coffee taverns survived very long. And the number of converts to the questionable delights of temperance was negligible (though the Salvation Army, at least, was able to win a few sober souls for God).'

One of the consequences of the Coffee Tavern movement was that coffee itself became part of working-class fare, but, as Jack London pointed out in the depiction of his turn-of-the-century journey into the destitute quarters of the city that bore his name, what was served up to the workers as coffee tasted pretty awful.

❖19❖

THE COFFEE ZONE

THE TROPIC OF Cancer is that imaginary line circling the Earth at approximately 23.5° north of the equator which marks the northern boundary of the geographical region known as the Tropics. The equivalent line marking the southern boundary is called the Tropic of Capricorn. Both are now misnomers as they were named over 2000 years ago when the sun was pointed toward the solar constellation of Cancer during summer solstice and the constellation of Capricorn during that of winter. Since then the earth has moved on in its celestial wandering so that really we should be talking about the Tropics of Taurus and Sagittarius. The fact that we don't provides us with a curiosity of the human mind: some things have a logic; others have a logic as long as it suits our purpose.

Coffee grows best in the tropical zone, not because of the heat but rather the light, which lasts longer inside this zone than on either side of it. The coffee plant doesn't like too much heat, which is why the best coffee is grown in mountainous regions or else in areas well protected against the extremities of sun.

With the right technology and care, coffee can actually be grown anyplace, a possibility that the Eden Project has capitalised on by selling coffee plants over the Internet to hundreds of caffeine-obsessed people who not only dream of roasting but also growing their own. It's a mug's game, however, and except for having an aromatic mascot, growing coffee at home is of little use if a drinkable cup is what you're after. The coffee plant knows where it likes to grow – and it's not on the windowsill of a snowbound flat in Brooklyn.

The Coffee Belt is that zone spanning the globe between Cancer and Capricorn. It's here all commercial coffee is farmed. Almost every viable plot of land inside this zone has grown coffee at sometime or another. It takes in the Americas – where coffee is grown from Mexico down through Central America to the bottom of Brazil, the Caribbean and Hawaii (the only place in the USA that grows commercial coffee); Africa – including the coffee growing countries of Ethiopia, Uganda, the Ivory Coast, Tanzania, Kenya, Cameroon, Congo, Burundi, Rwanda, Guinea, Togo, Zambia, Zimbabwe, Nigeria, Ghana, Malawi, Gabon and Benin; India, Indonesia, the Philippines, Vietnam and the very southern bit of China.

When we consider that even by the mid-1800s coffee was grown commercially in only a few select regions, the explosion of coffee production that took place at the end of the 19th century seems astonishing – especially as the many new coffee growing countries produced beans almost exclusively for export to Europe and North America.

But in the last decades of the 19th century, two important things happened that contributed to this change: coffee leaf disease began decimating major production areas in the East – primarily Ceylon, Indonesia and the Philippines; and the coffee culture in Europe and North America was being spurred on by technological advances that created a vast new market for coffee consumption. So the consequent coffee shortage – that even the mighty Republic of Brazil couldn't fill – was a strong inducement for new territories to try growing coffee and old territories to modernize their antiquated production systems.

It was also at that time that an important new player in the coffee trade came forward. The Germanies had been a major consumer and distributor of coffee from the very beginnings of coffee's entry into Europe; but it wasn't until late into the 19th century and the foundation of the German nation state, that they became involved in coffee production.

Unlike the other major European powers, Germany had no significant colonial possessions until then, concentrating instead on its domestic manufacturing and competing with England to be the world's workshop. But after the Franco-Prussian war in 1870, Germany became more outward looking and entered (reluctantly) into 'the scramble for Africa' – seeing it, from the perspective of the new economic order, as a necessary way to protect trade, as well as safeguarding access to raw materials and export markets.

Along with Belgium, Britain, Portugal and France, Germany carved out large areas of Africa, prospecting it for the best means of exploitation. Coffee quickly became one of the main items of interest when it was discovered that certain varieties were indigenous to sub-Saharan Africa where they grew wild and, most importantly, seemed resistant to disease. This discovery would have great implications in the decades to follow as botanical scientists struggled to find a cure for the voracious Hemileia vastatrix – commonly known as coffee rust.

The colonisation of Africa was very different from that of America. By the latter part of the 19th century the former colonial powers were using another language to justify occupation and exploitation of lands they acquired by whatever means available. The politicians now spoke of bringing the benefits of enlightenment to the barefoot natives – not so much by the cross and the sword but thorough secular education and the Gatling gun. Whatever language was used, however, the consequences were the same. Land was despoiled and cultures destroyed (or transplanted to European ethnographical museums). But the coffee trade prospered as various horticulturalists and agronomists in places like the Jardin Botanique in Brussels, the Royal Botanic Garden in Edinburgh along with state-run agricultural research centres in England, France, Germany and Holland, began to lend (or sell) their specialised knowledge to planters anxious to learn more about recently discovered coffee varieties. In the main, these new African coffee plantations were set up with more technological understanding and more technical skill at their disposal than those of previous generations. So African coffee farms – like Africa itself – became one vast laboratory for the coffee industry.

As well as in Africa, underdeveloped areas in South and Central America were given over to coffee production. How anxious these new nations were to establish a foothold in the buoyant coffee market can be seen in a report written in 1893 for the International Bureau of the American Republics, based in Washington DC, which talked of a rapid increase in consumption of coffee with rising prices indicating that supply is still below demand. 'These facts,' the authors concluded, 'have naturally turned attention to this industry in those regions where the coffee plant thrives, and has prompted many inquiries from persons seeking investment regarding favourable locations, prices of lands and general information upon the subject.'

The report then went on to give details regarding certain inducements various South and Central American countries were giving in order to lure North Americans and Europeans into immigrating for the purpose of helping to build their coffee trade. Venezuela, for instance, offered grants to all immigrants voluntarily coming to the country, including payment of passage, both by sea and land, along with board and lodging expenses for thirty days after arrival. Potential colonists were offered exemption from military service – an important consideration as most of Latin America was involved in territorial disputes. Also, special provisions were promised for individuals and companies wishing to organise colonies for settlement – an opportunity seized upon by a number of religious groups that felt oppressed in their European homeland.

Many German colonists, especially, took advantage of these generous offerings and settled in South and Central American countries in great numbers, soon becoming an important force in the coffee trade there. However, the links forged with coffee roasters and distributors in Hamburg would have eventual repercussions a few decades on when the United States joined sides with England and France in World War I, and tried forcing Central and South American coffee nations to sever relations with German nationals.

The Coffee Zone was divided into spheres of influence, if not by outright boots-on-the-ground colonisation. Coffee producing states of Africa and Asia might have been Europe's economic 'protectorates', but as the countries of South and Central American gained independence from their former overlords, the US began filling the vacuum

– adapting colonialism to changing economic conditions.

Of course, as the United States consumed far and away the most coffee of any nation in the world, its economic clout would have influenced political decision making in those states that depended on the US market to sell their goods. But trade advantages came at a price, especially as distribution was mainly controlled by corporate interests in the north.

The problem, though, for those in Europe and North America who sought control of the coffee trade, lay with the Colossus of the South. As Portugal had found much earlier, to its dismay, Brazil was just too big for others to manage.

If the Coffee Zone had a locus, Brazil was it. And where the coffee trade was concerned, it was Brazil that mattered most. This was something the new coffee nations hoping to cash in on a booming trade would find out soon enough, to their eventual cost: the Coffee Zone might have spanned the globe, but the price of coffee was determined by what was happening in Santos and in Rio.

However, something was taking place in Africa that was about to change the game. New seeds were being tested and new varieties of coffee grown. Coffea Arabica was about to have its competition in a rough and tumble relative that could grow twenty metres tall. Its name, quite appropriately, was Robusta.

INSTANT BUZZ

WAR HAS A lot to answer for, not the least of which is the creation of instant coffee. War speeds things up. So does caffeine. The two went together like sugar and cream.

The idea of instant coffee actually goes back a long way before Nescafé tried to take over the world. In the battle of the brews someone or other was always trying to get the essence of it bottled or tinned – both for the sake of convenience, as making coffee back in the 19th century was a time-consuming process, and because sometimes there simply wasn't a roasting pan and grinder readily available. As the coffee drink evolved from pleasure to habit to necessity, immediate availability became an issue.

From the point of view of the coffee traders, being able to sell the essence of coffee rather than the beans meant that nobody asked where coffee came from. By the time coffee was a standard item of sale in grocer's shops, people had become aware of the differences in taste between 'milds' and 'Brazils' (often a euphemism for 'rough') and, if they had a choice – though often, they didn't – opted for Mocha or Java, which meant 'smooth'. As coffee was usually mislabelled – and who was to know? – being told where it came from didn't really mean much, unless you were lucky enough to have a coffee merchant living next door. But as time went on, more people became savvy about buying beans and opted to purchase them from tradesmen they could trust.

Selling the essence of coffee, rather than coffee itself, avoided a lot of tricky issues. It could be stored indefinitely without loss of quality, since quality wasn't the question. And it could be consumed anywhere, anytime, without need of special paraphernalia.

So, from the very beginning, instant coffee was understood both by traders and producers to be the magic bullet that would someday give the coffee business unlimited reach into, then, unreachable markets. It wasn't coffee lovers these merchants were interested in. People who loved coffee were already hooked, knew where to buy it and how to prepare it. The dealers were after the masses of people who didn't care about coffee itself, had never actually tasted decent coffee, and simply wanted a caffeine buzz.

The first successful 'instant' coffee was hardly coffee at all. Created by Paterson & Sons of Glasgow in 1876, Camp Coffee was barely five percent coffee essence and twenty-five percent chicory in a solution of sugar water. It came in a flat-sided glass bottle affixed with a label that depicted a seriously kilted Scots soldier sitting outside his tent, sword at his feet, holding aloft a cup and saucer. A turbaned Sikh servant stands at his side, holding a tray containing a bottle of Camp and a pitcher. In the background are the rugged cliffs of a snow-white mountain with a banner stuck at the very top, emblazoned with the words, 'Ready Aye Ready'. The text on the label reads 'Camp Coffee and Chicory Essence'. And in small letters at the very bottom of the label are instructions to mix a spoonful in a cup with boiling water and cream.

How much of this stuff actually made it onto the battlefields of India, Afghanistan, Sudan or wherever else the British army fought in those years, is open to question – though one might assume quite a lot as the product lasted up until the present day (though now it seems to be used primarily for adding flavour to pastries and cakes).

I remember an old friend telling me how he grew up drinking Camp and didn't have real coffee until he went to Paris as a young man. He remembered the flavour with childhood affection – which probably says more about the distorting power of memory than of the physiology of taste buds. Although, I suppose with enough sugar we can learn to like anything.

There were many attempts at trying to get a soluble form of coffee that captured the aroma and taste of a freshly brewed cup – an impossibility, of course, but since access to real coffee was still limited, for many people there was nothing to compare. Coffee, however, is a very delicate substance; if it isn't treated right it gets bitter, like a petulant child. Once ground, it deteriorates quickly when left out in the air, therefore it needs to be brewed and consumed soon after granulation. So capturing that moment of goodness and saving it intact for later consumption was quite a challenge.

The first commercial breakthrough came in 1901, at the Pan American Exhibition held in Buffalo, New York, where a small booth was set up by Kato Coffee Company. A leaflet handed out at the time read, 'Satori Kato is the name of a scholarly Japanese who after many years of research and study has succeeded in discovering a process for the condensation and purification of coffee. The great value of this discovery is made apparent by practical demonstration at the booth, Sec. J. Liberal Arts Building.'

Japanese-born American chemist, Dr. Satori Kato, had developed a dehydration process for making soluble coffee at the behest of an American coffee importer. The result that was first put on public display at the Exposition in Buffalo, was then marketed through a Chicago company set up under Dr. Kato's name.

Reading over the advertorial bumph that the Kato Coffee Company used to introduce their instant enterprise is fascinating and instructive, if not a bit comical. Early coffee ads felt obliged to state the obvious, since people had yet to be inundated with the commercial barrage that later generations learned to ignore unless presented with candy-coated dreams that spelled out 'happily ever after' in glorious Technicolor.

Kato Coffee's promotional information began by focusing on the economics, claiming that their extraction process reduced ordinary coffee to one-tenth its weight – but emphasising this small fraction contained more actual cups than in a full pound of beans. Also, less sugar was required (still a costly item in 1901), 'owing to the withdrawal of the rank and bitter elements.'

Then they pointed out the ease of preparation: 'Kato Coffee requires neither roasting nor grinding. A pure, fresh and delicious cup of your favorite beverage is at your command at "a moments" notice. It requires no expert cook to prepare it; a child can produce the same result as an adult.' (Note the sequence of key adjectives: 'pure, fresh, delicious'. Truth in advertising was no more an issue in 1901 than it is today.)

Another matter they addressed was the avoidance of mess – a supposed concern of turn-of-the-century housewives or at least those imagined by Kato's copywriters: 'Kato Coffee, is made cleanly. It may safely be made in your parlor or in the midst of your gathered friends at the social board. It leaves no grounds.'

Health issues were touched upon as well. Kato assured their potential customers that all the deleterious properties of coffee had been eliminated, such as: 'The woody fiber (or coffee grounds) which are indigestible, the rancid fats, that lead to so many cases of Dyspepsia, and above all, a greater portion of the caffeine, known to the medicinal world as — The Arch Enemy of the Nerve System.'

And who would use it? Kato Coffee listed them out, exclaiming that their instant product 'will prove a marvel of convenience to the Housekeeper, the Bachelor, the Soldier or Sailor, the Explorer, Traveler, Hunter, and for Camp Life, in fact, to the lover and drinker of coffee the world over, owing to the simplicity of preparing the beverage.'

How about that?

Curiously, the booth where Kato Coffee Company was prophesising a new world of instant, dyspepsia-free coffee was right around the corner from the Puerto Rican exhibit which was touting some of their very fine Arabicas grown in the Yauco mountains by Corsican immigrants since the early 1800s. President William McKinley, a coffee lover who was known to friend and foe as 'Coffee Bill', had stopped by to sample a cup of the Puerto Rican variety shortly before he was assassinated. Whether American history would have been rewritten had McKinley tried Kato's instant instead is unlikely.

In 1910 an instant coffee company was founded by a Belgian immigrant to the United States with the very convenient name of George Washington. Washington had studied Chemistry in Germany at the University of Bonn and had lived in Guatemala where he would have come in contact with the large community of German coffee planters. Having hit upon a process of making instant coffee, Washington set up shop in New York City.

The G. Washington Coffee Company was a well-funded operation that projected a 'real American' image rather than one of exotic oriental, even though Kato had probably lived in America longer than Washington. But this theme of 'Americanism', which was often a coded term for white, Christian, European, played well in the run-up to World War I – even though by 1914 Washington's German links would have been problematic should they have been made public (though having the fortuitous name of 'George Washington' provided excellent cover).

World War I, however, gave G. Washington Coffee a splendid opportunity to imbed its product within a closed community of desperate soldiers who found the bitter taste of this soluble gunk fitted in quite well with life in their rat-infested trenches: it kept them awake enough to appreciate the pure horrors of war.

Washington Coffee used their war credentials to good advantage after the troops came marching home, unemployed but victorious, trumpeting its slogans on posters and in ads: 'Went to War and Home Again! Supplied to the boys in the trenches because the Government wanted them to have the best. Now that it is home again, you can have the best!'

One of the devices G. Washington Coffee used to convince people to buy instant coffee despite their many reservations was linking it to the zeitgeist of modernism. Instant coffee was the wave of the future and the future was now. Interestingly, they hit upon the metaphor of sugar as a way of connection: 'Do you know that there are millions of people who have stopped using the ground bean? Back yonder everyone used whole brown sugar – without refining – now everyone uses refined, white granulated sugar. In the same way, millions have stopped using bean coffee, with its messy grounds – and are using refined coffee, made by Mr. G. Washington's special refining process. G. Washington's coffee is just as superior to whole bean coffee as modern white sugar is to old-fashioned brown sugar.'

Heavily refined, white granulated sugar had been sold to the public as better than brown (just as over-refined white bread had become 'better' than whole wheat) because it was white, and white was the colour of purity, and because it was easily soluble. This combination of purity, solubility and modernity was a powerful triumvirate in convincing the American people to make the switch from real to instant. There was only one problem – it tasted horrible.

It took the combination of two more significant events to push instant coffee into the mainstream of consumption: problems in Brazil and another world war.

The economic crisis of 1929 found Brazil with vast stockpiles of coffee sitting in overflowing warehouses, unsold and unwanted. In desperation, millions of coffee beans were either burned or thrown into the ocean by government fiat in a last-ditch effort to protect the plummeting price of upcoming harvests. Vast fortunes were lost in the coffee trade. But in Switzerland, this worldwide disaster was looked upon as just another financial opportunity.

Nestlé, had long wanted to expand their commodities empire of condensed milk and chocolate. The company, based in Switzerland, which operated factories in the United States, United Kingdom, Germany, and Spain, was one of the pioneers in using highly professional and well-organised scientific research laboratories to develop new technologies for the food industry.

World War I created a demand for powdered dairy products that Nestlé was quick to provide. But the end of the war and the return to fresh milk saw their profits plummet, so the company was keen to develop new products for the post-war market.

The crisis in Brazil, along with Nestlé's analysis of global coffee trends, convinced them that there were excellent prospects investing in cheap coffee if they could create something that up till then had eluded even the most brilliant scientists – making a soluble form of coffee that actually tasted good.

Having previously developed a technique for dehydrating milk that was used in the manufacture of milk chocolate and powdered dairy products, they seemed to have the technology required for success. The task, however, was more complicated than they had imagined.

The company commissioned a young chemist, Max Morgenthaler, to head the project of creating a coffee extract powder that they hoped would set a new standard for instant brew. After seven years of failed attempts, Morgenthaler finally achieved the desired results by spray-drying liquid coffee under high pressure to create a rich, soluble powder and the first drinkable instant yet produced. In April 1938, Nescafé was finally launched – just in time for World War II. So, again, it was war and the American armed forces that gave instant coffee, phase 2, a boost as packets were provided for soldiers' daily food rations.

Nescafé became the first truly successful instant coffee distributed widely on a global scale. As its home office was situated in the neutral country of Switzerland, Nestlé avoided the difficulties of embargos and boycotts imposed on the Axis nations and the countries they occupied. But, even more, the agreements which Nestlé reached with Brazil whereby cheap coffee was contracted for processing into long-lasting instant that could be warehoused, shelved or sold any place at any time, paved the way toward a commodity chain under corporate control that was to become so important in subsequent years.

The impetus in launching soluble coffee as a major commodity on a global scale may have been an overproduction of Arabica in Brazil, but it was Robusta that instant liked best. This simple fact suddenly gave coffee's ugly ducking a purpose and, curiously, paved the way for the control of the coffee trade by the giants of the processed food industry. Once people accepted instant coffee as an alternative to freshly ground and freshly brewed, it followed that highly capitalised and highly efficient corporations would be the ones to benefit as only they could bear the cost of production on a massive scale.

On the other hand, instant coffee, no matter what we might think of it in terms of taste, helped to expand the market into areas where coffee had rarely been consumed – such as rural communities in the Chinese hinterland. This further globalisation of coffee consumption spawned new areas of production in countries like Vietnam, with huge harvests dedicated almost entirely to the Asian instant coffee trade.

Instant coffee was brought about both by need and desire: the need of a coffee industry bursting at the seams and desperately searching for new and more lucrative horizons; and the desire of an ever anxious populace to find a ready boost for energy exhaustion. The brave new world required instant buzz and a spoonful of brown powder mixed with boiling fluid in any kind of cup provided a quick and easy fix for midday slumps when a five-minute break was all that was on order. But for those many who became hooked on this artificial high, savouring the beauty of the bean in its gastronomic glory was, sadly, denied them. Instant coffee along with instant mashed potatoes and instant noodles in a pot, unfortunately defined a post-war generation. No wonder the children of the cultural revolution that followed turned it all on its head, making freshly brewed espresso into an obsession.

❖21❖

COFFEE IN CRISIS

FARMING BY ITS very nature creates an economy of boom and bust; some years are good and harvests are bountiful, some years are bad and crops fail to flourish or wither on the vine. This sequence of feast or famine is often hard to predict for most cultivation. But coffee is different. There is a rhythm to its growing cycle that ordinarily means a bumper harvest is followed by one of scarcity. As the crop is harvested twice a year and in so many countries of the world, adequate supplies can usually be maintained if one takes into account the ease of storage – under proper conditions, green coffee can be warehoused for extensive periods without affecting the quality. So, in the natural scheme of things, coffee supplies could be evened out allowing for stability in pricing. That, of course, is before the arcane world of commodity trading enters the picture.

The coffee business had always been difficult since its very inception, especially in the early, colonial years; the difference, as economies evolved, was more in the abstraction. When coffee was commoditised (along with all primary crops like sugar, cotton, wheat, etc), it became an entity that existed beyond the actual plant. As such, the idea of a seed from a living organism was replaced by a concept relating more to a roulette chip than to a coffee bean. What this meant in practice was that decisions influencing the coffee trade, and thus the lives of both producers and consumers, were often made without regard to the product, but simply to numbers that were generated on endless rolls of ticker tape.

In 1893, the *New York Times* ran a story about a man named George Kaltenbach, a German national living in Paris who had engineered a roller coaster ride on the coffee market whereby he was able to purchase a million bags of coffee at one price and sell them on at a price 40% higher a short while later. The reporter who wrote this story for the *Times* may have been horrified at the power some European gentleman could wield over the US coffee trade simply by means of a telegraphic connection to the other side of the ocean – accomplished, one imagined, with a casual nonchalance while supping in some lavish Parisian hotel on truffles and champagne complete with a demitasse of café Bourbon. But the man from the *Times* needn't have gone so far afield; similar dealings were taking place all the time back home in New York and Chicago.

New technologies not only made change possible – such as allowing a transatlantic futures trade – they also made change necessary. The building of railways that opened up the coffee farms deep in the Brazilian hinterlands allowed harvests to reach the docks in a matter of days rather than weeks. But having built the rails, certain areas were favoured over those that still relied on mules to carry produce over the mountains. Therefore it became necessary for all farmers who wished to compete in the export market to have access to rail transportation.

Better storage techniques meant green coffee stock could be protected from mould, mildew and a myriad of other problems besetting bags of beans that lay in wait for market prices to shift. Improved ocean transport brought coffee speedily to receiving depots in the key consuming nations, allowing supplies to be readily accessible on site rather than held back in less-than-adequate warehouses at the various ports of embarkation. So, once established, coffee growers had to tie themselves into this commodity chain no matter how it affected past relationships based on collaborations that went back generations.

Advanced communication devices also became a necessity of trade, forcing administrative centres to relocate along the primary trunk lines that carried the coded messages so vital for instantaneous decision-making. Early in the 20th century, it still took longer for telegraphic information to reach coffee traders stationed in New Orleans than New York because of the delay in transmission; so even though New Orleans was a major coffee port, coffee traders had to move their main offices to New York City simply because the five or ten minute delay in getting pricing news could have meant a significant loss in potential earnings.

But, most importantly, the modernised industrialisation of coffee had implications about the way it was produced, the consequences of which were not always in the interests of the growers or consumers. High finance always had its own agenda of maximising profit and made demands accordingly. Rationalising production as a requirement for further loans hardly ever benefited small and medium-size farmers.

Primitive techniques in preparing the coffee bean for market, were cheap but inefficient. However, it meant that small farmers could prepare their own coffee for export in a way that best suited them and their particular conditions. Once the more technically advanced equipment was available, it was demanded by foreign coffee merchants in order to maintain what they perceived as a standardised quality in coffee production.

Since the new technologies required significant capital investment, small growers essentially lost control of their harvest, as the berries were sold on to large pulping factories often owned and run by major distribution concerns financed by foreign interests. All this gave further power to American and European companies, allowing them more leverage over every phase of the coffee industry through advances on future harvests and loans for equipment upgrades.

It was, of course, the coffee republics that suffered most. Boom and bust economics meant that great wealth was mirrored by massive poverty. Since there was little domestic consumption in the coffee producing regions, the national economies that were bound to the coffee trade in the Americas, Africa and Asia, found themselves trapped in global business cycles with little control over the harvest price their growers might achieve from one day to the next.

The question of 'free trade' as opposed to structured markets – or, in the parlance of the consuming nations, 'protectionism' – came to a head as the 19th century turned into the 20th. A series of bumper harvests in Brazil caused a coffee glut that threatened to impoverish the coffee growers by dint of plummeting prices for beans that were becoming more expensive to harvest than could be recouped through sales.

In an attempt to protect the Brazilian coffee industry, in 1906 the government established what was known as the Coffee Valorization scheme. Essentially this was a way of propping up coffee prices and guaranteeing an income to growers by means of a government subsidy, whereby bumper harvests would be purchased and stored until the world market had recovered. From the perspective of coffee planters in Sao Paulo and Rio, the valorization scheme was successful but it inevitably led to a global oversupply when warehoused coffee was released and therefore escalated the impact of the inevitable economic downturn.

Of course, Brazil was far from alone in supplying the world's coffee. But even though the other coffee growing republics in America were suffering from the same crisis of economic strangulation by an unregulated commodity market, the coffee barons of Brazil (and it was the very wealthy Brazilian coffee merchants who set the valorization scheme in motion) would just as well have seen Colombia, Guatemala, El Salvador and all the other upstart coffee producers pulped in their own fermentation tanks rather than build a pan-American defence in support of a fair pricing structure.

Brazil won few friends and allies in its isolated power game. Even though it had gigantic muscles to flex, the nation's control over coffee production was limited as the interconnection of global finance and the multinational nature of the commodity trade had already created a neo-colonial dependency.

As often happens in moments of crisis, it was the small farmers who suffered most. Those who had the backing of large capital either survived the loss and went on to make another fortune when times were good again, or else they turned their restless minds and bountiful wallets to other things. For many of the wealthiest plantation owners, the coffee business was simply a way of making money from what seemed to be a good investment – as trading in addictive drugs is usually quite profitable if one is able to weather the occasional whirlwinds. The others, the small growers for whom coffee was both their life and livelihood, had no option but to continue even if they had to sell their produce at a loss – or see it go up in a fiery blaze of caffeinated misery.

In June, 1932, *Time Magazine* ran a story scandalously headlined, 'Brazil: Destroy! Destroy!' The article, angry and terse, read: 'Ruthlessly resolved to force coffee prices up, Brazil's National Coffee Council promised to burn a total of 18 million sacks each containing 132 lb. of coffee. At approximately $6.50 per sack, $117,000,000 worth of coffee will have been turned to smoke and ash. Never before have men burned so much that is good to drink!'

With the onset of the Great Depression, coffee producers found themselves facing a dramatic fall in international prices, precipitating a economic crisis that had been brewing since early in the century. As a consequence of the valorization program, overproduction continued unabated as growers were still compensated for coffee left unsold. In an act that some saw as one of desperation but others perceived as sticking two fingers up to the shadowy world of commodity trading, Brazil embarked on a crazy adventure that, in the scheme of things was bound to fail, but made the rest of the world sit up and take notice by means of a surreal form of epic theatre. Millions of tons of coffee were set ablaze in ceremonial bonfires; millions more were dumped dramatically into the ocean. Brazil, in 1932, was covered in a burnt umber haze of vaporised espresso.

The coffee-drinking nations of the north were aghast. In London, New York, Paris and Berlin images of coffee beans piled high in mounds that looked for all the world like giant funeral pyres, filled the pages of newspapers with a kind of curious titillation. Was this a form of national mass suicide or an act of blatant hostage taking, with the collective bean in the role of a coffee-starved consumer? (Interestingly, the *Illustrated London News* focused on Brazil's more creative use of transforming excess coffee into a national asset by pressing the beans into bricks and utilising them instead of coal to fire steam engines bringing ever more coffee from farms a thousand miles away back to the glutted warehouses of Santos or Rio. Trains then must has smelled wonderful!)

Coffee growing remained in a state of crisis for the rest of the decade with a climax reached in 1937 when over 70% of Brazil's coffee stock was destroyed. It wasn't until the Second World War and after many thousands of farmers had yet again been brought to the brink of starvation in the face of economic madness, that a real attempt was made at creating a structured market which would establish a fair price for coffee harvests no matter where they were grown.

In 1940, the coffee producing countries of America agreed to a quota on their harvests if the United States accepted a restriction on its imports. This resulted in a sustained increase in the price of coffee that lasted until the mid 1950s. In 1963, the International Coffee Organization was established to administer versions of this agreement on behalf of the major coffee producing and consuming states. A target price and quota system lasted, shakily, until 1989 when it finally collapsed under the renewed free market mantra of the coffee consuming nations led by the US. And, once again, the coffee growers were left to fend for themselves.

A few years back Benoit Daviron and Stefano Ponte explored the apparent contradiction of a coffee crisis in producing countries along with a coffee boom in consuming countries which created a widening gap between producer and consumer prices. They called this 'The Coffee Paradox.' And certainly a paradox it is. But coffee has been around for quite a long time now, and so have countries like Brazil. The evolution of product and demand has been a bumpy road with many twists and turns, some obvious and others quite unexpected. In the end, however, it's people who grow coffee and it's people who drink it. When the two come together – the grower and consumer – it's a powerful combination. How this happens, how this process of connection can be explored, provides the basis for conceptual unravelling of an apparent paradox and replacing it with an alternative vision of cooperative endeavour. Whether this is possible in the face of uncompromising corporate greed is something else again.

Bricks of coffee used as fuel for locomotives in Brazil

22

Espresso!

IN JANUARY 1941 an article appeared in the *New York Times* entitled 'An Ode to Empty Cups' which captured a bit of doggerel that went: 'When in Rome a King held sway, I drank coffee every day. An Emperor he became as well, still I sniffed the coffee smell. When he seized Albania's land, even that mere smell was banned. If Benito stays, I know, even the coffee pot will go.'

Whether or not Italians were actually singing this mournful song in the harsh winter of '41 or if, more likely, it was a creature of the invisible minister for war propaganda, World War II left Italians coffee deprived. Even as far back as 1939, Mussolini's government was urging the people to reduce coffee consumption, barraging them with desperate slogans which aimed to convince a caffeine starved populace that they should return to the customs of their ancestors; rhetorically asking, in scornful tone, 'Did the Romans drink coffee?'

But for all their bravado, the Fascist government knew coffee was a vital commodity for Italians and the lack of a steady bean supply was bad for morale. In fact, Mussolini's plan for a new Mediterranean empire included the coffee rich regions of North Africa where thousands of Italian colonists were encouraged to settle. However, it wasn't as easy as the legions of old; Ethiopians in particular were less than accommodating and barefoot Abyssinians countered Mussolini's military might with extended guerrilla actions which included destruction of coffee plantations.

Unwilling to use their precious gold reserves to purchase ready supplies of coffee from South America, the Italians had tried bartering with the coffee producing nations trading military equipment, including submarines and fighter planes, for beans. The supplies they gained, however, were far from sufficient to satisfy demand and by April, 1939, a strict rationing regime was in force that limited individual purchases of coffee to seven ounces. By 1941 even that pittance was gone and coffee was essentially unavailable except through black marketeers who brought in haphazard supplies by way of Switzerland.

Coffee didn't return to Italy's grocery shelves until 1946. After a caffeine drought of nearly seven years, Italians were more than ready to renew an enduring romance with their favourite beverage. In the ravages of their war-torn country, cafés with coffee machines that had been coldly collecting dust began to come alive again with a long forgotten zeal. Coffee was back. The nightmare had ended.

The Italian post-war economic miracle was caffeine charged. No matter where the money to fund it came from, nor the Faustian bargain made, the Phoenix rose once more. From flattened cities with starving kids to a level of prosperity never before witnessed, Italy was on the move. And few things symbolised this extravagant energy as much as espresso.

Italian espresso was more than a drink; it was a way of life. The brew, the special roast and the machines that extracted its essence, connected not only to the gastronomic sensitivities of a population bred on taste as an alternative religion, it also harnessed the energies of communal creativity which had been stifled so terribly by Italy's dalliance with Fascism. What's more, it allowed a renewed bond with the nation's greatest resource – the Italian diaspora.

A 1927 study by the Italian government estimated that over nine million of its citizens were living abroad—one fifth of the entire nation. Vibrant Italian communities had been set up throughout North and South America, Oceania and Africa. Even more communities could be found in Britain and throughout the continent of Europe.

Unlike many immigrants who broke ties with their past and their native homelands, Italians tended to maintain strong connections with their country and their families who remained on Italian soil. Not only did these overseas Italians provide money through remittances sent to relatives back home, they also formed a nucleus for distribution of Italian goods and services.

By the end of World War II, Italian communities in cities like San Francisco, New York, London and Melbourne had re-established links that had been closed off during the conflict. Within a few short years, the war (with Italy, at least) had been forgotten and people whose lives had been put on hold for the duration, if not shattered by the brutalities of battle, rushed to rekindle dreams that had been temporarily forgotten. Artists, writers, painters, poets were energised to make the world anew. It was a time of flowering, a time to let loose after so many years of misery and hardship.

Unlike Italy, people in the English-speaking world had coffee during the war, as the supply line, especially from South and Central America, had never been cut off. But coffee in Britain and North America, at least, was a bog standard, instantised drink that was used more for its effect than its flavour. War-time coffee had little allure except as a habitual substance which could help induce wakefulness. Italy, on the other hand, had hardly any coffee but the little they possessed was cherished and consumed like the finest of wines. There they brewed coffee with care and with pleasure.

And so it was the overseas satellites of the Italian motherland that launched the love affair with coffee and spawned the Espresso Generation in North America, Britain and Australia. But it wasn't only the drink; the post-war cultural explosion of youth that found its home in the Italian style café were just as intrigued by its centrepiece, the device which made it all possible – *la bella macchina.*

The espresso machine was almost as much a symbol of the age as the brew it created. Able to provide hundreds of cups of powerfully aromatic coffee every hour, it gave instant gratification while extracting an essence that had rarely been savoured before. It was new, it was beautiful, it was chic and exciting. It was big, bold and shiny. It hissed like a magic dragon behind a curtain of ethereal steam. It had gigantic levers pumped by proud Italians who were like Dionysian gods to the pimple-faced kids who gathered inside these new temples of modernity inspired by shots of sugared caffeine.

Not that the machine itself was new. Prototypes had been constructed much earlier in the century. What was new, however, was the technology which allowed for a more efficient system of pressurised extraction without scalding the coffee and embittering the brew. The creation of Signor Gaggia was a process which circumvented this problem by using steam to force a separate flow of properly heated water through the grounds under extreme pressure whereby a unique essence was discovered, a special extract which came to be known as 'la crema', coveted by Italian connoisseurs and ignored by most British and American coffee drinkers for whom the finer details of a coffee extraction was hardly what they were after – as it was all covered up by a blob of steamed milk anyway. What mattered to the young artists, writers and rebels who flocked to the bustling Italianate cafés in San Francisco's North Beach, Melbourne's Carlton, New York's Village and London's Soho was the froth and the espresso-charged atmosphere. The places might have been defined by the substance, but it was the buzzy ambiance that mattered more than the coffee they consumed in gallons once they got there.

Back in Italy, the post-war coffee bars were teaming while outside the motor scooters revved. The cafés of the Italian communities overseas were as foreign to them as they were to the Inuits of Greenland. For an Italian in Italy, a good crema mattered. You stood at the bar, downed a doppio and gave thanks that the war was finally over and you could have a decent cup of coffee again.

23

RISE OF THE GLOBAL COFFEEHOUSE EMPIRES

IN THE EARLY 1970s I was living in San Francisco's Noe Valley district which was then a reasonably priced, outlying area of the city populated in the main by older German and Irish-American families who found the cultural shifts happening around them quite bewildering. At the time, the neighbourhood was in the midst of a slow transition from a relatively stable nine-to-five, fried eggs on toast community to one that was more transient and dislocated: a mixture of students and youthful wanderers from Middle America swept up by the free-spirited winds of change blowing across the continent.

Noe Valley's main shopping thoroughfare, 24th Street, could have been in any comfortably working-class, urban neighbourhood with its combination of useful things and kitsch, more down-to-earth than fashionable, where café waitresses wore white aprons and knew the names of their customers sopping up bottomless cups of morning coffee while suffering through various degrees of heartburn.

One day a sign on an abandoned butcher shop advertised the coming of the neighbourhood's first coffeehouse – a fact that was greeted with joyous anticipation by the young domestic immigrants who had recently arrived and sheer horror by the old-timers who, quite literally feared their neighbourhood was going to pot.

The Meat Market Café, as it came to be called, was the brainchild of a young man by the name of Curtis Chan, who, himself, represented the shift in cultural values that had been emerging over the previous decades. Bright and energetic, of Chinese ancestry, he was quintessentially San Franciscan, combining the elements of integrated diversity that made the city such a vibrant and exciting place to live back then.

The café, itself, was modelled around the Italianate espresso bars of North Beach – and yet it wasn't. Certainly there was the Bella Macchina in all its steamy glory; however, though the coffee and the coffee apparatus may have been Italian, the place that served it up was 1970s California hip with lots of ferny greenery, mismatched tables and rickety chairs.

From day one the place was a roaring success because the artsy and rebellious youth who had taken up residence in this hidden valley that had yet been discovered by the moneyed classes, related more to a caffeinated bohemia than the hedonism of a Haight-Ashbury drug scene, and so were waiting for it to happen – even if they weren't quite sure what form 'it' would take.

In a magical act of transformation, the building once used as a butchery became our neighbourhood espresso café, communal and welcoming. The old refrigeration room where the carcasses had been kept was partially dismantled with just half a wall remaining that defined a more cosy and intimate space. Even the rail built into the ceiling which ran from the refrigeration room to the serving counter, where sides of meat had once been suspended on massive hooks, was kept as sort of a gruesome reminder as to the Meat Market's origin while accentuating the double entendre. Except it wasn't gruesome at all; the place was flooded with books, newspapers, journals, works of art, intimate conversations and romance. The Meat Market was buzzing with the energy of youth, which easily superseded the aura of dead cows; it was more like fashioning life out of death as the '70s were transforming the comatose '50s – or so we all thought.

The Meat Market café was just one of a number of neighbourhood coffeehouses springing up at that heady time in '70s San Francisco. Based in emerging communities of political and cultural disenchantment, they were islands of sanctuary and resistance that provided a space for exchanging ideas, fantasies and propositions, challenging old notions and confronting new ones. They were centres of a blistering world of intellectual and artistic reconstruction, peopled by wide-eyed refugees from a confused America, tiptoeing into the unknown and fuelled by Italian espresso that was becoming more and more fused with elements from its adopted home as time went on.

These new American espresso cafés paralleled a seismic shift in worldly visions that defined the 1970s and the great social and political upsurge that was happening then. Not only did they begin popping up in cities along the Pacific and North Atlantic coasts, but also in university towns throughout the country as shifting populations, anointed by the bean, brought the love affair with the new coffee culture they had discovered in San Francisco, Seattle, Boston and New York.

The first ripple of espresso that trickled across America in the late 1970s was hampered primarily by one thing – even though the cafés had been Americanised, the method of brew remained something of an Italian monopoly in so far as the equipment and its maintenance were controlled by Italian companies that combined leasing their machines with service contracts which even included coffee supplies. Therefore setting up an espresso café in the American hinterland was often both costly and problematic, as equipment frequently broke down and spare parts could be difficult to obtain.

But as the emerging coffee culture developed, it became clear to anyone who experienced the excitement and energy of American espresso café life in that amazing decade when all things were deemed possible, that it was only a matter of time before an enterprising visionary (or wealthy speculator) would find a way to franchise a McDonald's-type espresso operation and set up shops in every village and town from Pocono to Dixie.

It actually took longer than I would have guessed at the time for a Starbucks to materialise. Even though there were no end of Johnny Coffeeseeds who, out of a desire to launch 'the next big thing', sought a way to bring espresso to the masses, the challenge was enormous. The reasons it took so long, however, were both cultural and economic.

The coffeehouse movement of the 1970s was the absolute antithesis of the fast-food franchised world that had grown so rapidly in post-war America. Epitomised by industrial style chicken and hamburger chains that had surfaced in all parts of the country and catered especially to the long-distance drivers lost on endless highways who wanted food in sanitised surroundings that all looked the same, they symbolised a lot of what the young refugees from suburban America were rebelling against. The '70s coffeehouse culture, and the unique form of coffee served there, represented, if anything, a rejection of the values that spawned these clone-like instant food services.

But a decade on, things began to change as the political upsurge of the '70s became more quiescent in the '80s. The country had become more wealthy. Credit was cheap and easily obtainable. People bought houses for prices that were reasonable and watched as property values began to skyrocket, turning real estate into assets that they dipped into like bottomless saving accounts. Young professionals moved back into the cities, abandoning the suburbs. And suddenly leases for storefront properties began to mount.

Once property became expensive, the independent cafés that were located in many urban neighbourhoods found themselves in trouble. The almost communal atmosphere that could be maintained when rents were cheap now became subject to the laws of economics. Some cafés survived this difficult process, others didn't. Those that did had to walk the fine line between having a free and easy espresso café and running a business that, if not making a profit, could still pay its monthly wages.

The story of Starbucks exemplifies the curious connection between the '70s ideals of the early American espresso movement and the worldwide coffeehouse conglomerates that became such a remarkable phenomenon. Whether one looks at it as just another form of economic colonialism or an inevitable result of timely opportunity, the history of the company's founding and development is both fascinating and instructive – and, as with all allegorical tales, comprises currents that often flow counter to the way we might expect.

The original Starbucks was an offshoot of the idealistic coffee movement that swept the west coast of America in the 1970s. However, this early venture wasn't based around espresso but rather the connection with real coffee and the basics of brewing techniques that had been re-discovered in places like the San Francisco Bay Area.

In fact it was in Berkeley that Starbucks claims to have found its model in the form of a gourmet coffee grocer, an immigrant from Holland rather than Italy, who prided himself on purveying freshly roasted premium beans to customers who had grown up drinking instant stuff or brewing stale coffee from nondescript origins that had long ago been crammed into a can.

Starbucks was first launched when the founders moved north to Seattle and set up a store based on the idea that people who were interested in real coffee would want to buy it freshly roasted, freshly ground but brew it themselves at home. So the original shop, more a bean market than a café, didn't even have an espresso machine. It was only in 1987 that the forerunner of the Starbucks that we identify now as the global espresso goliath came into being.

The founder of Starbucks Mark II, Howard Schultz, grew up in Canarsie, a working class section of Brooklyn, New York. In his curiously titled book, *Onward: How Starbucks Fought for Its Life without Losing Its Soul,* Schultz writes about his background growing up in semi-poverty after his father was laid off from his delivery job as a consequence of an accident which left him incapacitated. According to Schultz, his difficult upbringing led him to crave both financial success and, if success was granted, to run a 'responsible' company that would treat its employees better than the terrible way his father had been treated.

Born in 1953, Schultz was of the generation that came of age when the first wave of espresso hit the urban American sub-culture. However, going to university at Northern Michigan in Marquette, a rather small port town on Lake Superior which must have seemed like a million miles from nowhere to an eighteen-year-old from New York, it might not appear surprising that his first experience with espresso came, he says, when he visited Milan, Italy in 1982 and was blown away by the number of cafés serving this exceptional coffee drink. It was there he conceived of his mission to bring the wonders of espresso and its miraculous effects back home to America.

However, by that time Schultz had been working at the original Starbucks as a marketing and buying rep for several years and Seattle, in those days, already knew of espresso. Certainly, if he had travelled down the coast to San Francisco – as he must have done – he would have discovered a vibrant espresso culture in North Beach every bit as exciting as that of Milan's, even if in miniature. So why Schultz's Italian experience became his epiphany is somewhat baffling, unless one takes his little vignette as perhaps it was meant to be taken – as part of an apocryphal tale that establishes ownership of an idea purporting to be reality. In this case the idea – or the impression Schultz was trying to sell – is that the American espresso culture was somehow invented by Starbucks; a notion so patently ridiculous that when I first grasped the implication, I could only stare in awe at the brazen chutzpah of the man.

Yet, beyond the flagrant balderdash, there is an element of integrity about what Schultz was trying to do – or what he says he was trying to do. He wasn't putting his energies into yet another fried chicken empire that took millions of crated chicks pumped full of hormones, covered them in salt and sugar and tried to force-feed them to the nation's overweight citizenry. He claims that what inspired him was espresso's ability to stimulate community and his own desire to do good. So as well as achieving the American Dream of wealth beyond most people's wildest fantasy, he wanted to establish a company with ethical concerns regarding both those he employed and the product they served. That, Schultz says, was his intention. And I'm sure it was. After all, he came of age when young people were listening to songs by Bob Dylan and Phil Ochs – before the time that businessmen and financiers could claim quite openly that greed is good.

Setting up a chain of espresso cafés in the 1980s was a bold move as implicit in the idea was the notion that the drink and place it was consumed, so identified by the counter-cultural cafés of the

'70s where mainstream America dared not venture, could actually be made acceptable to the middle classes. But several things had changed along the way. America was yet again in a period of transition where the sharp divides of the previous decades were starting to become blurred. In the interim, young rebels had become thirty-somethings and were beginning to take the notion of 'career' more seriously than before. Whereas in the '70s people wore a self-proclaiming badge on their chest, in the 80s it was becoming harder to tell what side of the fence people were on simply by looking at them.

Perhaps Schultz's vision in Milan of a espresso culture that drew in ordinary people from all walks of life was more prescient than many had thought. In central Milan, the cafés were sparkling clean, glitzy and, at the same time, homey. But that, of course, was Italy. In America, the coffeehouse was still associated with a type of youthful grunge. Off-putting to the mainstream Jane and Joe, perhaps, but whether they would have felt more comfortable in the mirrored cafés of Milan is questionable.

Prior to taking control of the original Starbucks in 1987, Schultz had started his own espresso outlets which he had called Il Giornale as a testament to his love affair with Milan. The cafés were re-named Starbucks after he purchased the company from the original owners. That he chose the Starbucks name over the Italian brand he had created was an important decision. Taken from the classic novel,

Moby Dick, Starbucks was a word that native English speakers could easily pronounce. More than that, it set the tone: espresso might have come from Italy (as did Columbus), but it would only reach its true potential, Schultz came to believe, when it became American – so Il Giornale dissolved into Starbucks.

Seattle of the 1980s was the perfect place to launch the Starbucks home-grown espresso venture. In many ways it had a similar history to San Francisco as a West Coast port city that had grown wealthy in the gold rush. But it was also that much further north, closer to Canada than California. Even more subject to the cycles of boom and bust than its southern counterparts, it was still recovering from the recession accentuated by cutbacks of its major employer, Boeing Aircraft, which had been suffering from the after-effects of the global oil crisis.

The flip side of this downturn, however, was that property had become reasonably priced again. And with a skilled labour force of highly trained technicians, a well-developed urban infra-structure and a cityscape that was every bit as beautiful as its distant California neighbour, 1980s Seattle resonated with a similar magnetic appeal as San Francisco did in the 1960s. Except it wasn't displaced children with flowers in their hair who were drawn here – instead it was educated professionals who were following the new technologies along with those Californians (known as equity refugees) who sold their property at a sizeable profit and bought homes three times bigger and four times cheaper in the Pacific Northwest.

As so often before in coffee's curious history, the buzz of change meshed well with the buzz of caffeine. And the wired-up, energised life-style of 1980s Seattle was fertile ground for Schultz's new venture of launching an easily replicated format that would bring espresso, if not to the masses then to the new techno-savvy labour elite along with the cosmopolitan middle-class who had both money and time on their hands.

It probably took someone like Schultz who knew about coffee from his years at the original Starbucks, who knew about corporate organisation from his years at IBM and who knew about the nitty-gritty of life from his years in a Brooklyn housing project to put all the pieces of the jigsaw together and actually make it work. Coffee doesn't take kindly to either ignorance or mistreatment. But, then again, since the vast majority of Americans still hadn't tasted coffee any better than store-bought instant, the bar wasn't set very high.

Starbucks was never going to take the place of community cafés where a counter-culture of one form or another was looking for a communal space that had a unique identity and a large enough following to pay the rent. Nor could it compete with the cafés that prided themselves in quality coffee and had a clientele with palates educated enough to tell the difference. But Schultz was clever enough to see that there was a new market for espresso in the wider population who wanted a clean, well-lit space to have a quick high-powered drink that speeded up their day.

Seattle was Starbucks' proving ground. But its real success story lay elsewhere. Knowing his potential customer, what they looked like, where they gathered, meant Schultz could fix on possible locations where white-collar workers or middle-class shoppers with a bit of extra money in their pockets could pop in for a quick espresso drink, heavily laden with foamy milk and flavoured with syrups like amaretto or grenadine, without feeling any sense of not belonging there – because Starbucks would be downtown, right next to stores like Macy's and Burger King; and if not downtown, then tucked away safely and securely in a gated shopping centre.

That espresso had become mainstream cool and no longer a sign of cultural rebellion was emphasised a few years on with television sitcoms like Friends, where the coffee café became the hub for the pretty child-like adults who shared their soap-opera dramas on the soft furnishings of their local coffeehouse with a mug of some sort of caffeinated drink in hand. They all had decent jobs – or were about to get one – money in their pockets and wanted little more from life than a nice hot drink, innocent fun and willing, sexy friends. These, I suspect, were the photo-fits of the imaginary customers Starbucks had in mind when they tried to project their identity.

However, being savvy businesspeople, they knew the difference between image and reality. A shot of espresso could also provide a temporary lift out of the emotional depression that came from a growing sense of social alienation – which was probably more in keeping with the bulk of their eventual clientele.

The global coffee culture that Starbucks came to represent took American television and cinema as its cue. Even though it hadn't the actual equipment to replicate Hollywood's dazzling imagery, it based its allure on glamour by association. Between the end of the war in Vietnam and the beginning of the conflagration in Iraq, the United States still had a captivating pull on millions of dewy-eyed youths around the world who craved the Technicolor dream they saw unfold on the giant screens of their local cinemas. If some felt that to eat a McDonalds hamburger or drink a Starbucks latte was to vicariously taste the delights of a globalised future, that subliminal message had been transmitted to them in a million different ways through TV, music and films, created and packaged to sell and promote the good life a fantasy America could offer.

In 1987, Schultz had six shops in Seattle and had expanded his operation to Vancouver and Chicago. By 1989 he had 46 stores and by 1992, when Starbucks first went public, there were 140 throughout the US. In 1994 that number had doubled and the market value of the company was worth almost a quarter of a billion dollars. In

1996, Starbucks opened its first location outside North America in Japan and two years later took over 65 shops in the United Kingdom. As of 2012, Starbucks had over 17,000 stores in North America and countries throughout Europe, Asia, Africa and Central and South America. In 2013, the company was estimated to be worth over 32 billion dollars.

From the home of social and political opposition to the realm of cultural acquisition, the multinational espresso industry of the 21st century became a by-product of a very curious set of circumstances whereby a drink of empowerment was appropriated by the very forces it once, symbolically at least, stood up against. There were no conspiracies; what happened was simply the logical consequence of a globalised economy where a company from one nation calls the shots because it has the money and the power to do so.

Independent cafés, however, were not – as has sometimes been suggested – crushed by companies like Starbucks. Of course they couldn't compete for the same clientele on the same turf, but just as the coffeehouse movements of the 1970s evolved from a need and desire for a dislocated community to connect, so have they today. In a multitude of exciting and inventive ways, new spaces have been carved from relics of the old, transforming worlds through the magical wonder of the liberated espresso machine – as the Meat Market did those many years ago.

24

COFFEE CULTURES OF THE FAR EAST

A WOMAN ENTERS a café. The place is full up – no seats are vacant. A hostess greets her and takes an order for a drink. The woman stands and waits patiently for an empty table while consuming her flavoured latte. She waits, ten minutes, twenty minutes, half an hour. No one budges. Embarrassed, the hostess delivers the woman another drink, free of charge, and apologises profusely for the inconvenience. Finally someone leaves and the woman is escorted to a table where she will sit, reading, writing or playing on her computer. The seat is now hers for as long as she wants it.

The country is Japan, the city is Tokyo and the café is one of a large Western chain – with a very different twist in its tail. The international corporate coffee culture may have arrived, but with an overlay that's distinctly Japanese.

Throughout the Far East, in all the major urban centres – whether it be Singapore, Beijing, Tokyo, Seoul, Jakarta or Manila – American and European coffee chains are thriving in shopping districts awash with garish signs promoting the brand names found along the universal avenues of every global metropolis. Tourists feel comfortable there, as do the native residents who want to connect with the electric buzz of London, New York, Milan or Paris without paying the price of international airfare. But to see these entrist organisations as simply a rubber stamp version of franchised culture replicated over and over again, down to the last coffee stain on a white logoed cup, masks another reality equally important: adaptation happens with humans as it does with plants.

When Westerners think of coffee it's not the Far East that immediately springs to mind. In fact it comes as a surprise to most people in Europe and the United States that Vietnam is the second largest coffee exporting country in the world – perhaps because most of the coffee produced there goes directly to China, which is not noted as a coffee drinking nation.

It's true that coffee became popular in Europe long before it was a drink of consequence in most of the Far East, but in countries like Malaysia that had a large Muslim population coffee arrived very early on by way of merchants who travelled there from Arabia, Turkey, Persia and India. Other Asian nations had coffee imposed on them by colonial powers: Indonesia by the Dutch in the 18th century; the Philippines by the Spanish in the 19th century; Vietnam by the French in the 20th century. But however coffee arrived, indigenous coffee cultures eventually took root and developed a unique relationship with the societies that embraced them.

In Singapore, for example, though the Western

coffeehouse scene is flourishing, there is a parallel world of indigenous cafés specialising in local coffee – kopi. The coffee served is pure Robusta roasted in palm oil mixed with maze and sugar – decidedly an acquired taste but loved by the pre-Starbucks generation. As the cost for coffee at these cafés is barely half the price of a cup at one of the Western coffee chains, business is booming. Small, independent kopi cafés selling soft-boiled eggs with runny yolks, kaya toast buttered thick with coconut jam and steamy cups of their powerful coffee concoction still have more appeal to native Singaporeans than the glamour of chocolate sprinkled cappuccinos and gilded muffins.

Likewise in the Philippines, even though the youth are bewitched by Starbucks-like coffee emporia, the elders still fancy a cup of Barako – when they can get it, as the true Liberica beans that give this brew its special kick are often in short supply.

Ironically, the Philippines was once a major coffee exporter. At the end of the 19th century, during the Spanish occupation, the islands were one of the largest producers of Arabica in the world. Then, as in Ceylon and Java, they were hit by a plague of Hemileia vastatrix and, almost overnight, the coffee industry was obliterated. Farmers began to sow replacement crops and what remained of the coffee growing areas were replanted with hardier varieties – Robusta, Liberica and Excelsia – which had the ability to better withstand the virus. But the Philippines lost the Arabica trade, which their coffee industry had been based upon, and other countries in the region, such as Vietnam, were better placed to take advantage of the growing commerce in non-Arabica varieties.

It might have been Robusta that the industry wanted for their booming instant coffee trade, but it was Liberica that Filipinos had somehow come to love. Native to the small African state of Liberia (itself a curiosity of nations), the Liberica tree produced a bean considered harsh in flavour and irregular in shape that was hardly attractive to the global distributors. To Filipinos, however, its harshness signified vitality and power and so they called it Barako, the Tagalog word for 'manliness'.

The small Filipino coffee farmers who were growing these varieties in the mountain areas of Batangas, Cavite and Apayao found themselves in a difficult position. Without capital to set up processing factories and distribution networks they were at the mercy of the corporate giants who wanted only Robusta for their soluble coffee trade, which even at rock bottom prices provided a steady, if meagre, income.

However, the domestic demand for real Barako survived. Abandoned Liberica coffee orchards were rediscovered and cultivated for the internal market and the many thousands of Filipinos living abroad who still crave this curious coffee product.

I find it fascinating that the wild Liberica coffee tree, first stumbled upon by former American slaves who were shipped back to Africa to colonise a bit of their ancestral homeland, somehow made its way to the Philippines, itself colonised by Spain, a country heavily involved in the slave trade, and later by multinational enterprises whose original fortunes were made through plantation slavery. How fitting then that the harsh bean from the Liberica tree, which many Filipinos grew to love (so contrary to the current obsession with the mildness of Arabica), became such a symbol to them of cultural independence.

On the Indonesian island of Sumatra, in the northern region of Aceh where the coffee drinking tradition goes back many hundreds of years to the time when Arab traders first arrived, meeting over a cup of strong black brew in small coffee shops and stalls has long been part of the daily routine of village men. During the period of conflict in the 1980s and '90s, coffee shops, it is said, served as sort of a neutral zone where the Free Aceh Movement and the Indonesian military could imbibe their morning drink openly without fear of either side opening fire. In fact, male villagers often found it safer in coffee shops than in their houses where they might have been hunted down by soldiers searching for insurgents.

Aceh is the only province of Indonesia to apply Islamic Sharia law, which is why the cafés there were a male bastion. But something quite remarkable happened in December 2004. A devastating tsunami hit Aceh and many aid workers from various parts of the world descended on the region. As quite a few of these aid workers were women who took up residence in towns and villages to help with reconstruction, the coffee shops quickly changed their men-only policy in order to accommodate these gallant volunteers. Now, according to the *Jarkata Post*, coffee shops in Aceh cities are no longer closed to women. Many female customers ranging from housewives to teenagers frequent the shops for a bit of caffeinated refreshment. Mothers even bring along their children.

Most of the coffee brewed in these cafés is sourced locally from growers in the Central Highlands. Some of these varietals, like Gayo coffee, have developed a unique international reputation. The preparation also seems to be peculiar to the region. Water is poured through grounds held in a cloth sieve several times in succession and collected in a large bowl and then, like Moroccan tea, poured at some distance into glasses, thus aerating the brew and causing it to froth.

There are suggestions that the strong taste and aroma of Aceh coffee comes from grinding marijuana leaves into the blend – an idea that is not at all preposterous as cannabis is often used as a flavour enhancer in local cooking. If true, however, it probably gives the coffee an extra lift and might explain its former use in mediating Aceh's civil conflict.

Coffee came to Japan quite a bit later than to Indonesia even though now its per capita consumption is greater than any other country in the Far East (or even Australia and Great Britain). But, as Japan had effectively closed itself off to Western customs well into the 19th century, the coffee culture there is relatively recent. Up till then it was only a small section of the population that came into contact with the drink through the Dejima trading post off the coast of Nagasaki which provided the single place of direct exchange between Japan and the outside world. Dutch ships were the only European vessels allowed to harbour there and even they were under strict quarantine and heavily guarded.

But after the Meiji Restoration of 1868 the nation underwent a rapid industrialization that turned Japan from an agrarian society into a major industrial power within the course of a generation. As a consequence, many peasants found themselves landless and impoverished, creating a pool of displaced agricultural labour which eventually became the basis for the turn-of-the-century Japanese diaspora and the subsequent connection with the global coffee trade.

This connection was attained by a curious synchronicity of events. Brazil, which had finally abolished slave labour, by law if not in practice, needed workers for the massive expansion of their coffee industry. In the latter part of the 19th century, Italian peasants who had also been uprooted from their ancestral lands had filled this shortage. However, treatment of Italian immigrants by plantation taskmasters more used to dealing with human chattel than contracted workers had been so brutal in the transition years from slavery to free labour, and tales of systematic abuse so horrified people back home, that in 1902 Italy enacted legislation prohibiting subsidized immigration to Brazil.

Previously, Brazil's white elite had restricted entry of non-Europeans (unless brought in as slaves) but economic necessity trumped racial nonsense and so in 1908 the country opened its doors to Japanese immigrants, who came there in vast numbers. Many of these immigrants eventually became coffee farmers themselves and, like the Germans in Central America, provided a commercial link to merchants back home.

Even earlier than Brazil, in the 1890s Japanese began to settle in Hawaii finding ready work in the coffee trade. By 1914 more than 80 percent of the Kona coffee crop was produced by the Japanese and by 1931 over a thousand Japanese families were identified as coffee growers there.

Japanese immigration to both Brazil and Hawaii thus helped stimulate a brisk coffee trade inside Japan throughout the 20th century, only suspended briefly during the war years. This opening of new markets for coffee also happened to coincide with a great change in Japanese society as the industrial boom had created an affluent middle class anxious to taste all the strange and exotic fruits that had been so long denied them.

The Brazilian-Japanese connection was underlined by one of the first of what was to become a great wave of coffeehouses that would soon spring up throughout Japan. Café Paulista, named after the region in Brazil most noted for its coffee farms, opened on Tokyo's Ginza in the first decade of the 20th century. The Paulista introduced the educated middle classes to the delights of caffeinated stimulation that went beyond the mannered sipping of green tea and quickly became the haunt of Japanese artists and writers who ardently took to this mix of European and South American culture.

Coffee entered the Japanese mainstream quite easily as it followed on from established networks of teahouses, though it quickly separated itself off from them. The Japanese coffee shop, known as *kissaten* or *kissa*, soon could be found in practically every Japanese town. Mainly family owned, each *kissaten* prided itself on brewing its own special coffee from a variety of techniques and having its own unique identity. Tucked away on side streets or in alleys, they had a homey atmosphere where residents – mainly men – could linger, read the daily papers and chat. Unlike Western cafés of the period – especially in Britain and the United States – Japanese *kissaten* were said to brew excellent coffee. Some even roasted their own beans on the premises.

The urban *kissaten* were more cosmopolitan and frequented both by men and women. They often catered to particular interests such as music, literature or art. The *meikyoku kissa* or classical music café – specialised in specific styles of music and even specific composers. Others had walls lined with books of certain literary genres where readers could drop by, drink coffee and discuss the latest trend or ponder some esoteric composition that excited the new generation of youth who seemed to be making up for all the time lost in not-so-splendid isolation.

The Japanese coffeehouses evolved, as did the society, shifting their appeal as fashions changed from one thing to another. But after the terrors of the Second World War in which the country was cruelly devastated, the energised reconstruction that followed ignited a parallel coffee culture which, in Western eyes, defined Japan's relationship with coffee more than the *kissaten* because it seemed so incredibly bizarre. Coffee in a can dispensed by the ever-present vending machine came to be stamped on Japan's post-war identity like Godzilla films and Manga comics.

It's rather sad that the delights of the *kissaten* have been so overshadowed by this very peculiar Japanese form of 'espresso' – this quick, take-away hit of milkified caffeine that spoke of the Bullet Train and the *oshiya* station attendants who had to stuff riders into impossible spaces, just as coffee was.

The South Korean city of Busan is just a short ferry ride from the Japanese port of Fukuoka where the southern tips of these two countries seem to snuggle up and kiss – though 'kiss' might not be the most appropriate metaphor. The Japanese occupation of Korea from 1910 through the Second World War left bitter feelings of resentment; however, the Japanese did bring the culture of the *kissaten* to Korea which launched the country into a never-ending love affair with coffee and cafés that has yet to be satiated.

In Korea the original coffeehouses were called '*dabangs*'. Coffee however was very expensive for ordinary people to consume, so cafés were often based around cheaper commodities like tea, soup and kimchi. Even in the 1960s coffee was hard to get because of incredibly high prices and government restrictions.

As a divided nation which had come to symbolise the ideological chasm splitting the post-war world into competing camps, the role of the café in Korea became similar to the European experiences during civil and economic crises where the café itself was generally suspect of being a place of potential, if not actual, sedition. It's hardly surprising, therefore, that the Korean café became a popular and important place for young people to congregate and express themselves through various clandestine means by way of art, music and literature, fuelled by caffeine.

Coffee is now central to the café system in South Korea. As the country has become quite affluent, the drink is affordable to a large section of the population (even if the cost is ridiculously high). Koreans have developed a taste for artisan coffee and are brewing some of the best Arabica money can buy.

In recent years, the Western coffee culture – and especially that of the United States – has become quite influential in South Korea. But, as elsewhere in Asia, the Koreans have managed to expound on the theme and morph it into their own. Remarkably, the communal societies of the East have managed to develop their special take on the inherent individualism of the European and American café and create a space that is unique to them. At first glance it might look the same to most Western visitors, but in fact it's very different.

Of all the Eastern coffee cultures that have emerged over the last century, Vietnam's is perhaps the most remarkable. For those who came of age during the American incursion in the 1960s – over which time almost 12 million gallons of toxic defoliants were sprayed across the region polluting rivers and streams as well as vast swaths of farmland – the amazing reconstruction that took place over the last few decades has been astonishing to witness.

Coffee came to Vietnam by way of the French who brought seedlings from their plantations in Reunion –

the Indian Ocean island once known as Ile Bourbon. Experimental farms were set up in the Tonkin region near Hanoi at the end of the 19th century, but it was found that the Arabica variety didn't grow particularly well there, mainly due to soil conditions. This was around the time when the coffee rust disease was laying waste to farms in Java, the Philippines and Malaya. It was decided, therefore, to plant the hardier varieties – mainly Robusta.

Nowadays a wide variety of coffees are grown in the rich soil of the Annamite Plateau in the Central Highlands but the vast majority is still Robusta, used primarily as an export for the instant coffee industry but quite enjoyed by the Vietnamese themselves through their own unique method of brewing.

There is an active coffee culture in Vietnam based around a multitude of small coffee cafés throughout the country. Traditional Vietnamese coffee is prepared at the table using single-cup metal filters called '*phin*'. Coarsely ground coffee is tamped down and held in place using a perforated 'spreader' and the *phin* is set atop a cup that contains a few tablespoons of sweetened condensed milk, customarily used in many parts of the tropical Far East as fresh milk spoiled so quickly in the blistering heat. Boiling water is then added and the brew is allowed to drip very slowly into the cup, a process that requires patience – unlike the immediacy of European espresso. The head of the largest Vietnamese coffee company was once quoted as saying that for him watching the slow process of coffee dripping from the *phin* into the cup was an act of meditation – something offset by the buzz of finally drinking it, I imagine.

Coffee provides most of the country's primary export income. As of April, 2012, Vietnam had nearly 1.3 million acres of coffee under cultivation, 94 per cent of which was family-run farms of three to four acres (comprising, in total, more than one half million farmers). But while Vietnamese coffee has a 20 percent market share of world coffee exports in terms of volume, it earns only around 2 percent of the total revenue because the country sells unprocessed green beans directly to large distributors like Nestlé which uses them to manufacture instant coffee powders.

A government report in 2012, suggested that the country was in danger of losing much of its trade in the next 10 years if coffee trees weren't replanted, as almost 50% of the trees can no longer produce good harvests due to heavy use of pesticides and chemicals. The Ministry of Agriculture and Rural Development, along with conservation groups such as the Rainforest Alliance, is working on a strategy for more sustainable growth in the future. One can only hope, for it would be a sad irony if the devastation to the land caused by decades of war would be continued by blinkered economics.

❖25❖

CHINA

THE STORY OF coffee in China is complex. As much as one might try to squash the nation into a box labelled 'tea drinkers', the idea of writing any generality about China is similar to summing up the evening sky. The question for both is where do they start and where do they end?

Statistics collected by the International Coffee Organization indicate that people in China only consume .01Kg of coffee per year. That, of course, tells us very little since in some parts of China people hardly drink any coffee at all and in others they drink quite a lot. Also, whom are we talking about in a country made up of 1.3 billion people and 56 distinct ethnic groups? Are we referring to those who live in Shanghai or Beijing or the ones who reside in the autonomous region of Xinjiang Uyghur? Perhaps we might contemplate the 500,000 Europeans, Americans and Africans who live on the Chinese mainland. And if it's only ethnic Chinese we want to consider, should we include the 50 million expats who live in places like San Francisco, New York, Melbourne, Paris, London, Johannesburg, Sao Paulo, Manila where they've created their own little Chinas imbued with a Western coffee culture?

It's tempting to compare China with Japan. Both tried to isolate themselves from the world outside to a greater or lesser extent. Both tardily emerged from feudalism. And both catapulted themselves into modernity with a speed that was dizzying. Both were identified strongly with tea. Both sent forth a massive army of bonded labourers into the unknown – a diaspora, exploited and dehumanized; learning first hand about coffee's rude allure. But Japan was able to maintain its independence, while China, after the mid-19th century, was essentially gobbled up. The coast of China, that is; the Chinese hinterland was always, as it remains today, a world apart.

So if we consider simply the People's Republic as currently defined – a great land mass occupied by quite a lot of people who try to speak a common tongue (along with a multitude of other languages) – we find no general coffee culture as we have found in Japan with its history of the *kissaten* or even Vietnam with its unique tradition of coffee service. But we do find quite a lot of coffee drinkers and scatterings of strange coffee-related events as well as various localized cultures that hark back to a not-so-distant past. More than that, we find the future.

There was a curious coffee culture that existed in certain Chinese coastal cities from around 1860 through the early years of the 20th century as a result of the Opium Wars which, for a time, forced the country into economic subjugation. Treaties forced on China by the great Western powers ceded them enormous swathes of land. These so-called 'concession zones' gave Britain, France, the United States, Russia, Austria, Germany, Italy, the Netherlands and Belgium, along with Imperial Japan, rights to carve up the Chinese coastline and build extravagant replicas of their cities in miniature. These settlements drew in traders, entrepreneurs and vagabonds from around the world hoping to personally benefit from the enormous trade opportunities that had opened up in just a few short years where shiploads of goods were being siphoned out of China with the voracious force of a whirlwind.

The Europeans who populated these extraordinary districts within China had extra-territorial powers allowing them to pretty much do anything they pleased. And one of the things that pleased them was drinking coffee. In Shanghai, for example, along the Bund, the area of International settlement, there were European theatres, parks (with signs that infamously stated 'No Dogs or Chinese Allowed') and, of course, coffeehouses.

A special quarter of the International Settlement in Shanghai was the Restricted Sector for Stateless Refugees. Also known as the Shanghai Ghetto, it became home to 20,000 European Jews who were seeking asylum during the 1930s. One of the few areas where ordinary Europeans and Chinese co-mingled, it became noted for having some of the more interesting, if seedy, cafés.

Unlike Japan, China actually grows coffee and has done so for well over a hundred years. The southern province of Yunnan had coffee farms started by the French in the latter part of the 19th century who found the climate, soil and topography better for Arabica than the Robusta grown in Vietnam's central highlands, just across the border. So it's ironic that the coffee most consumed by the Chinese is of the instant variety made from Robusta beans, 95% of which are sourced from Vietnam.

Then there's Hanain, a semi-tropical island nestled in the South China Sea, stretching out toward the Bay of Tonkin, which has an indigenous coffee trade and where, on the south-eastern part of the island, people drink their morning coffee laced with coconut milk.

Fuijan, the province where la Roque's 17th century porcelain coffee cups had originated, grows coffee as well, though its commercial reach is still quite limited. Just off shore, however, lies the 'other China', Taiwan, where coffee production was taken more seriously. Arabica coffee trees were planted all across the island between 1927 and 1942, over 2,500 acres; not an enormous amount but a significant start for an emergent industry. Then came the war and coffee fields were converted to grain. It wasn't till the 1950s that coffee was grown again. Encouraged by industry reviews which showed Taiwan's Arabica beans to be of very high standard, production increased but costs were too high for

Taiwanese coffee to be competitive in a world market used to paying very little for its labour force.

The rapprochement between Taiwan and China, when business dealings began to take precedence over differences in ideology, allowed for the Taiwanese to bring their high-grade coffee plants to Fuijan, on the Chinese mainland, where labour costs were more in keeping with demands of the wholesalers – an extraordinary turn of events in light of the years when disputes over Matsu and Quemoy, the tiny islands claimed by both Chinas, took the world to the brink of nuclear disaster.

Coffee drinking in China is still seen as a Western lifestyle and more of a social trend limited to young, outward-looking urbanites who view it as their symbolic link to a globalised world. The European and American coffee chains play on this lure of the international marketplace, but a Hong Kong company is attempting to connect with a more typically Chinese style of consumption – both architecturally by furnishing their cafes with red blooming-lotus chandeliers and decorations in dark mahogany, and by adapting their drinks to conform with Chinese inspired flavours.

It's estimated that the total turnover of China's market for coffee shops hit over a half billion dollars last year and will triple by 2016. But as the cost of a cappuccino is even more expensive in China than in the States or Europe, consumption is mainly limited to the large cities. And many well-travelled Chinese consumers who have developed a taste for good coffee but shy away from over-priced coffee shops are starting to purchase single-origin beans to brew in their homes.

In 2012, the multinational food company, Nestlé, purchased over 10,000 tons of coffee beans from Pu'er, the largest coffee growing area in Yunnan, which produces the vast majority of all the coffee grown in China. Originally famous for its high-quality tea, Pu'er is undergoing a rapid transformation. The region currently has 70,000 acres of coffee in cultivation and is projected to have over 100,000 acres by 2015. This speedy rate of expansion has presented numerous problems, not the least of which is maintaining a certain standard of quality. But with such a high demand for Chinese grown coffee – part of an implicit bargain European and American coffee firms made with the government allowing them to trade there – the large coffee chains have been lining up to purchase supplies. Significantly, it was reported that in 2010, the CEO of Starbucks, Howard Schultz, flew in on his private jet for a visit.

Starbucks has shops in every major city in China – over 600 outlets in total, with 1,500 stores expected by 2015 when China will be the company's second largest market. Britain's Costa Coffee, which has three roasting units supplying its Chinese shops, is projected to have 500 outlets by 2016. And Pacific Coffee, Hong Kong's second-biggest coffee chain, plans to open as many as 1,000 stores, challenging both Costa and Starbucks in a market growing by 20 percent a year.

In stark contrast to the multi-national corporate descent on Yunnan, however, there is another and far more interesting coffee presence that has made itself felt in the region. Pioneers from various parts of the world have begun carving out a place for themselves in highlands of Yunnan. Youthful, energetic and often linked to global movements concerning ecology and fair trade, they have begun to link up with native growers, exchanging techniques and helping small farms establish cooperative processing ventures.

It is quite likely that in the near future these farms will connect with indigenous café movements starting to blossom in various centres of universities and arts where the coffee allure is strongest. A new and unique coffee culture is just beginning to develop within China; as it comes of age, the locus of the coffee trade will inevitably shift eastward.

❖26❖
VIRTUAL COFFEE, BIODYNAMICS AND ARTISAN CAFÉS

THE CHAPADA DIAMANTINA region of Brazil is a mountainous terrain halfway between the equator and the Tropic of Capricorn where the microclimate is ideal for coffee. There are a number of similar areas in the various coffee producing countries, but what is unique about Chapada Diamantina is that it boasts the largest collection of biodynamic farms anywhere in the world with over 600 workers dedicated to the pursuit of organic cultivation.

In an attempt to enter the European coffee market while still maintaining their biodynamic principles, several of the farms formed a co-operative enterprise to test the possibilities of direct marketing by partnering with an equally small UK based roaster and distributor. The elements of the project were very simple: to provide a source of additional income for the farmers, who were struggling to survive, and to make biodynamic coffee farming viable on a limited scale. Up till then biodynamic farming on small holdings was hardly practical in terms of individual farmers making a decent living or being able to provide investment for sustainability.

In order to accomplish these goals, the co-operative felt they needed to control the way their coffee reached the market. Modelling themselves on the idea of a farmer's bazaar where people could purchase directly from the growers, they attempted to subvert the distribution procedure that put the farmer at the bottom of the value chain. In contrast, the co-operative's model of direct marketing saw them involved in all aspects of production, distribution and sales, connecting growers to consumers half way round the globe.

Efforts like these have been duplicated in numerous ways over the last decade. Some have been successful, others not. Some are successful for a while and then fade away or morph themselves into something else. Often they depend on the energy of one or two dynamic individuals who may burn themselves out after years of swimming through bureaucratic treacle. What's important, however, isn't the aftermath of such ventures but the very fact that they've been attempted. If nothing else, they indicate to others what might be possible.

Connecting small farmers who grow specialty coffees and consumers who want to support sustainable agriculture is an idea that's both simple and powerful. Co-operative ventures like the one in Chapada Diamantina are becoming more commonplace. Sometimes it's been attempted from the other end. A number of independent cafés in the United States, Australia and Britain tried to seize the initiative and search out their own supply network, often making direct contacts with small coffee farms in El Salvador, Colombia, Ethiopia, Rwanda,

New Guinea and a hundred other coffee producing nations.

In London, for example, the Monmouth Café near Covent Garden has been making direct links with independent coffee farmers and roasting their own specialty coffees for several decades. Sometimes it's been small, regional roasteries set up by energetic young coffee enthusiasts, like micro-breweries in the real ale movement, that have become distributors to local independents and have provided the link between grower and consumer. Similar examples exist in Berlin, Tokyo, Melbourne, Prague and many other cities throughout the coffee drinking nations. These are the coffee idealists trying to carve out a sensible niche in the helter-skelter madness of the mainstream coffee world.

And madness it is and always has been ever since the early days of European mercantilism when coffee was produced through the most egregious form of chattel labour; when Haitian coffee plantations were angrily burned to the ground; when mountains of Brazilian coffee were dumped in the sea to protect pricing structures; when a lone speculator in Paris brought ruin to thousands by betting on coffee futures.

The coffee trade today is no less brutal if less bloodthirsty. Many thousands of peasants coerced into growing coffee have been left high and dry when large multinationals turn the screw one more twist toward poverty when supply outstrips demand.

It's not a bad idea to ask where something we consume comes from and how it got to us. It wasn't a bad idea to ask it in 1789 when French revolutionaries passionately debated the wording of the Rights of Man while drinking coffee that was harvested some months before by slaves who would continue to be slaves even after it was published.

But the coffee plant itself has often been mistreated. When the idea of produce is abstracted into a commodity that ignores its botanical essence, a problem is created similar to looking at labour as if it were an item on a spreadsheet rather than a human being of flesh and blood. When people have been abused to the limits of endurance, they rebel. Plants do so as well.

Sustainable agriculture is not just something to make well-intentioned greens feel good about themselves. It's simply a matter of respect for living things – both people and plants – and the understanding that treating them correctly is good for everyone. The opposite, when people and plants are mistreated, spells trouble. And trouble is the primary cause of stomach aches (for which, in Italy, strong coffee has long been seen as a cure).

In March, 2013, the president of the Central American Organization of Coffee Growers, was quoted as saying that coffee rust could reduce the year's harvest by twenty-five percent. A Guatemalan consultancy firm, Central American Business

Intelligence, estimated the figure to be closer to thirty percent and concluded that nearly one million Central American coffee workers would lose their jobs. In Jamaica, that same month, the president of the Agricultural Society said that thirty-five percent of the Jamaican harvest would be lost to a combination of coffee rust and the effects of Hurricane Sandy. And in Colombia, tens of thousands of growers and coffee workers took to the streets at the end of a strike which lasted for nearly two weeks, from the 24th of February to the 8th of March, 2013, demanding government subsides for uprooted fields.

Many farmer's organisations have blamed the outbreak of coffee rust disease on industrial practices that have been forced on them by wholesalers and processors (often one and the same) who demand use of pesticides and fertilizers which some farmers claim have weakened plant resistance to disease and lessened viability of the soil. The industry's response to this has been renewed efforts at creating disease resistant coffee varieties instead of focusing on essential soil nutrition and basic plant health strategies.

The crisis in the coffee industry has its historical precedents. What makes it different this time around is the incredibly rapid spread of coffee consumption which is increasing demand at a phenomenal rate. And the expansion of the coffee culture into China portends a shift in the locus of the coffee trade yet again – from Arabia where it all began, to Turkey, to Europe, to America and now to Asia.

But something else has changed as well. We have entered the realm of virtual coffee. An amazing plethora of sites including coffee junkies from all over the world spilling the beans, so to speak, on everything from their own predilections to promoting bad historical data that is lazily copied from one site to another, but also some amazing research and experimentation, sharing of resources and skills. YouTube videos show everything from how to use your popcorn popper to roast your morning coffee, to people growing diverse coffee varieties in their greenhouses, to lessons in picking berries from wild coffee trees and processing them yourself.

The lure of coffee has grown into an obsession. Coffee art is now something of a global sport with world-wide competitions (won in 2012 by a Japanese man who now has opened up a school for drawing intricate pictures in foamy milk). There is a massive number of people all over the world who have been educated in the subtleties of bean appreciation – which in turn has spurred an insatiable market for gourmet coffee. Artisan shops have sprung up in the most unlikely places. And, over the Internet, ordering can be accomplished by a simple click of the mouse and a bag of beans will be whooshed from Hawaii to Finland. It might be pricey but it seems those who've profited from new age technologies have plenty of dosh.

What does this mean for coffee's future? There have always been many coffee cultures that existed simultaneously. Coffee was harvested in the Ethiopian highlands by baboons even when Europe was drinking coffee harvested by slaves.

The idea of the café has also evolved. From the Penny University to Internet cafés where tourists check their emal and connect with other travellers, to the plethora of hybrid cafes in museums, bookshops, launderettes and bicycle shops. Coffee has found a multitude of ambiances and manners of consumption.

Virtual coffee has even gone one step further with the introduction of the 'gourmet' coffee vending machine serving espressos that promise to be just as good as your neighbourhood coffeehouse. (What that says about your neighbourhood coffeehouse is left unmentioned.)

With new coffee markets opening up to a massive trade, the crisis in coffee will reach extraordinary heights (or nadirs). The explosion in coffee consumption in countries with massive populations – China, India, Russia – has meant that the models of distribution and production are having to be quickly adapted. Coffee fields are being readied for a huge increase in supply. But since it takes four to six years for trees to produce their first harvest, the time frame always has a lag. And industrial coffee, as we have seen, is prone to major problems that can wipe out a crop overnight. Given these factors, we are dealing with unknown unknowns. Prices are bound to go higher as consumption increases and supplies shrink. And as the gourmet coffee trade becomes more important, the limited supply from small farms and fincas will tend to dry up. Costs will mount accordingly and good coffee will become like fine wine with people spending small fortunes for a bag of beans that promises untold delights in the fantasy world of affluent foodies.

Coffee, like other commodities, is going through a period of transition forced by economic, social and environmental issues. Questions of poverty in the developing world, health concerns, growing interest in pure foods and a demand for premium quality beans have combined to create a growing market for Fair Trade produce and organic coffees. The Internet has also become a major factor in educating and enticing consumers, expanding their interest in different coffee varieties and enabling small producers to distribute directly to customers through the World Wide Web. The future of coffee could very well be biodynamic with traditional varieties being grown on little inter-crop holdings and distributed directly to cooperative merchants for resale to consumers who will roast green beans themselves on open fires – thus bringing us back to the start of a cycle that began in the 17th century.

But the café will continue to exist as it always has. Coffee, the plant, has evolved in many and diverse ways. Shortages have historically been adjusted by either dilution or additives like chicory – which, as we have seen, some people have grown to love. And we will learn to grow coffee in many curious places.

What remain eternal are the need and the desire. The café space is a creative and inventive moment in time that empowers communal interchange. Coffee, historically, has been the perfect drink that allowed Sufis to commune with God, traders to commune with Mammon and artists to commune with their muses. The forms and nature of the drink and the place where it's consumed have been, and always will be, as fluid as coffee itself. But the beauty and wonder of coffee will continue to arouse the poet, philosopher, inventor and mystic who find the brew a means of entry into a hidden world of the mind – and the café, in all its wonderfully multitudinous constructs, will continue to form the milieu in which to share the magical discoveries inspired by the Black Apollo.

Notes

A WEBSITE HAS been set up as a companion to this book containing an extensive coffee bibliography along with images, charts, maps, statistics and discussions. It can be accessed at: www.blackapollopress.com/coffee.html.

The array of literature on coffee and cafés is boundless. In 2002, Richard von Hünersdorff and Holger G. Hasenkamp published *Coffee: A Bibliography* – a two volume set with over 1600 pages of multilingual references. But even such a monumental project, I suspect, only touched a small proportion of the coffee related material still hidden in small libraries and private collections throughout the world. The problem, of course, is that a good amount of the most interesting literature on the subject of coffee and cafés is included in works that are broader in scope and include intriguing references that are only discovered by chance.

However, there are some classic books that have helped inform our understanding of coffee history and the coffee trade, though less so on the subject of cafés and the integral relation these unique places of consumption had on the development of coffee cultures. The two main sources in English, both from the perspective of the coffee industry, were *Coffee: From Plantation to Cup* by Francis Beatty Thurber,

1881 and *All About Coffee* by William Harrison Ukers, 1922.

Much of Chapter 1, Delving into Origins, is based on Jean de le Roque's exceptional and very readable *Voyage de l'Arabie heureuse*, 1716. But the early years of coffee were mired in cultural misunderstandings and linguistic confusion. Ralph Hattox in his groundbreaking work, *The Origins of a Social Beverage in the Medieval Near East*, 1985, helped disambigulate centuries of preconceptions and attempted to build a more reasoned account regarding the initial development of the coffee culture in the Arabian peninsula and its expansion by way of Egypt into Turkey.

The Ottoman period, so crucial in the commoditisation of coffee as a secular drink, has been a subject of extensive research by a new generation of Turkish and Middle-Eastern historians. Some very interesting studies have made it onto the Internet which give a clearer insight into the amazing economic and cultural transformations that were taking place in Istanbul during this critical period. There are also a good number of more general cultural histories – such as *Istanbul and the Civilization of the Ottoman Empire* by Bernard Lewis, 1963 – which provide useful background reading.

The beginnings of Europe's fascination with coffee is best seen through the stories of the merchant adventurers from the East India Company and the Dutch VOC. I have found the reports and journals reprinted by the Hakluyt society especially useful. But there are also wide-ranging accounts by travellers and independent merchants – such as Leonhard Rauwolff, Pedro Teixeira, Prospero Alpino, Philippe Dufour, Jean de Thevenot, Ibrahim Pecevi, Olfert Dapper, Antoine Galland, Nicholas Blegny, Jean Chardin, and Carsten Niebuhr – which are readily available through various digital archives.

Coffee's entry into Europe is integrally connected with the shift in economic relations that were evolving in the 17th and 18th centuries. The best writings I have found on this subject have been by a group of social historians who pinpointed coffee as one of the key commodities that both accompanied and promoted this transition, like Fernand Braudel's *Structures of Everyday Life*, 1973, K N Chaudhuri's *Trade and Civilisation in the Indian Ocean*, 1985 and Kristof Glamann's *Dutch Asiatic Trade*, 1958.

The early colonisation of coffee – first by the Dutch and later by the French and English – can be seen from both above and below through the writings of the colonists themselves and the letters, journals and oral histories of those they colonised.

Café life in the 18th, 19th and 20th centuries is best explored through the literature of the various periods, especially as seen by the art movements and writers who frequented those special places of caffeinated dreams and incorporated the scent of coffee into their creations.

Much has been published over the last few years on the subjects of slavery, the commodity trade and the construction of the modern world. The development of the Brazilian coffee republic and its relationship to the emergence of other Latin American coffee producing states has also been well documented. I have referenced a number of these studies in the online bibliography but I found three collections of essays especially useful: *Coffee, Society, and Power in Latin America* edited by William Roseberry, Lowell Gudmundson and Mario Samper, 1995; *The Global Coffee Economy in Africa, Asia and Latin America, 1500-1989* edited by William Gervase Clarence-Smith and Steven Topik, 2006 and *Confronting the Coffee Crisis: Fair Trade, Sustainable Livelihoods and Ecosystems in Mexico and Central America* edited by Christopher M Bacon, V. Ernesto Mendez, Stephen R Gliessman, David Goodman and Jonathan A Fox, 2008.

The story of coffee is a wonderful example of what a double-edged resource the Internet has become in both providing access of information previously available only to a limited few and the flood of questionable data that is constantly being retransmitted as established fact simply because it's been published as such on so many websites. But the old adage of taking any received truth with a hefty dose of caution holds true in any medium of research.

Lightning Source UK Ltd.
Milton Keynes UK
UKOW04f2225051213

222502UK00003B/251/P